Carpenter's Children

. . . find and maintain . . . in perpetuity, four boys born within the City of London who shall be called in the vulgar tongue 'Carpenter's Children'. . .

From the will of John Don, relating to the bequest of John Carpenter, Founder of the City of London School.

Carpenter's Children

THE STORY OF THE CITY OF LONDON SCHOOL

Thomas Hinde

JAMES X JAMES

First published 1995
© City of London School 1995
ISBN 0 907383 483

New photography by John Spragg

Designed by Bob Speel

Printed in Great Britain by Foister and Jagg 1994 Limited

Published by James & James (Publishers) Limited
Gordon House Business Centre
6 Lissenden Gardens
London NW5 1LX

Picture acknowledgements:
The pictures on pages 11, 19, 20, 22, 23, 24, 35, 40, 52 and 91 are copy-
right Guildhall Library; those on pages 9, 10, 12, 13 and 56 are copyright
The Corporation of London Records Office; pages 15 and 17 are from
Tonbridge School; pages 57 and 58 from the Royal Institute of British
Architects; and page 122 from Tom Meddings. Many of the Chapter
Headpieces were obtained by John Fisher of Guildhall Library and are
copyright Guildhall Library. In the List of Old Citizens, portraits were
obtained from the following, who hold the Copyright: British Academy
(Sir Israel Gollancz), Bank of England Museum (Sir George Blunden),
Lord Judd, Gillian Edelstein (Julian Barnes), Professor Silverman, Lord
Snowdon (Sir Kingsley Amis), Crown Copyright\MoD (Sir Peter Levene),
Mrs Lewis (Professor D.M. Lewis).

Half title page: *The Milk Street School in 1867.*
Title page double spread: *View of the modern School from across the river.*
Opposite contents page: *The Embankment School in 1882.*

Foreword

I first met Thomas Hinde over meringues on the Concourse. CLS was playing host to visitors from Marlborough College, following that school's Commemoration Service at St Paul's Cathedral. I knew of him only as a novelist, but as we talked it emerged that he also writes school histories, has done so, in fact, for several of the country's leading schools. And, as they will, one thing led to another, possibilities turned to plans, concepts into contracts, and - an astonishingly short time later - here is *Carpenter's Children* ready to go before its public.

Since the tea-party, Thomas Hinde has become a familiar figure around the school, generally a little dusty from burrowing in the archive room, often deep in conversation with the Second Master, Terry Heard (Old Citizen) and William Hallett, Head Porter and Keeper of the Archives, both rich in CLS lore. I know that he would wish me to thank them most warmly for their support and advice at each stage of the book's production. (My own role, as is the way of Headmasters, was largely that of a bystander.) Valuable help has also been given by the Corporation's own archivists, now gratefully acknowledged.

Inevitably, *Carpenter's Children* owes much to Douglas-Smith's magisterial *History* of 1937. But whereas Douglas-Smith is exhaustively detailed and scholarly, Hinde's version brings the school to life with deft selectivity, compressions and an eye for the telling moment.

It demonstrates the school's unique constitution, its twin identity as an independent school (a founder-member, indeed, of the Headmasters' Conference) and yet, *pari pasu*, as a department of the Corporation of London, with all the benefits and difficulties of that ambivalent status. Much more important is this book's account of the true essence of CLS, its vigour, responsiveness to new ideas, cultivation of broadmindedness and the hard pursuit of both academic excellence and of the fun that life affords. The school is presented for exactly what it is, a microcosm of London itself, quirky, thrusting, sardonic and responsible.

Those who already know CLS and wish to know it better *Carpenter's Children* directs invitingly down the long corridors of time. For everyone else it is simply a very good read.

BRYAN BASS
May 1995

The New Buildings of the City of London School.

Contents

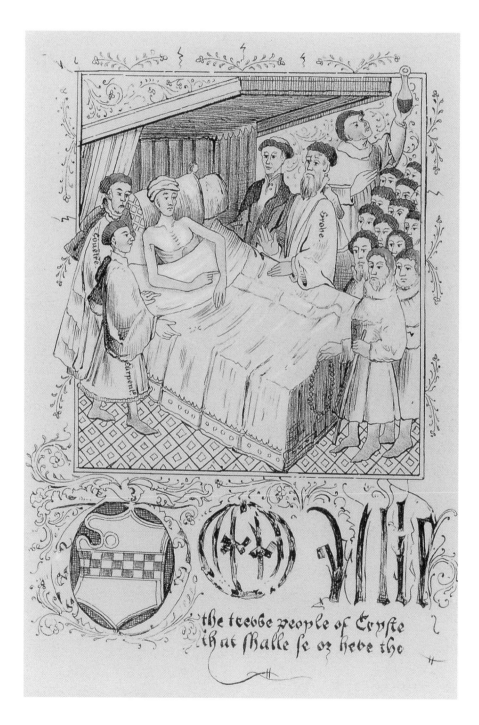

the trewe people of Cryste
that shalle se oz hebe tho

1

John Carpenter and the Missing Will

1442~1547

YOU CAN SEE John Carpenter, founder of the City of London School. He stands beside a canopied bed, as one of the executors of a dying man. There is no doubt that it is he, because his name is written vertically on his costume, just as the names of the other two executors are written on theirs. He is drawn as a short man (perhaps not to hide the executor behind him) with an unimpressive chin, but the gesture his hands are making suggests that it is *he* who is addressing the assembled company. The date is 1421 and the dying man on the bed is no less a person than Dick Whittington, four times Mayor of the City of London.

The illustration is the headpiece of the ordinances of a charity created by Whittington in his lifetime, which founded an almshouse for 13 poor men, one of them to be their tutor. All 13 are shown approaching the foot of the bed. Part of the duties of Carpenter and his fellow executors was to complete this foundation, and though the founding of such charities was not uncommon at the time, carrying out this duty may have suggested to Carpenter that he should establish something similar himself.

John Carpenter, sometimes known as Jenken, was an important man in his own right, Town Clerk of the City of London, at a time when the term clerk was a complimentary one, and when the merchants and manufacturers of London were becoming a power in the country. His statue at the School (which bears little resemblance to the figure at Whittington's deathbed) shows him carrying *Liber Albus*, a book of great historical value, setting out the laws, customs and privileges of the City of London. Today his compiling of this book seems his greatest achievement. In his time, however, his political and legal activities must have seemed equally important. In 1436 and again in 1439 he was elected to Parliament to represent the City of London.

His biographer, Thomas Brewer (from 1836 to 1870 the School's first Secretary) discovered other examples of the sort of matters in which Carpenter was involved. In 1437 he interceded successfully with the King's Council on behalf of the city of Norwich – which had been punished for anti-ecclesiastical riots by having

Opposite page: *The death of Dick Whittington.*

Opening pages from the Liber Albus *of John Carpenter*

Part of the Will of John Carpenter.

its liberties confiscated. In 1441 he acted as counsel for the City in the Court of Star Chamber in a case concerning six men who had taken sanctuary in St Martin's-le-Grand, but nevertheless had been arrested by the City's sheriffs. In the same year Henry VI granted him (together with two others, one of them the Chancellor of the King's Exchequer) a manor at Cheshunt in Hertfordshire, the annual rent to be one bow, value two shillings and one barbed arrow, value three pence. Ten years earlier the City of London had granted him an 80-year lease on the house that he made his home in what is now Leadenhall Street. For the first 30 years the rent was to be one red rose per year.

Brewer also discovered John Carpenter's will. Together with the will of his wife, Katherine, it provides further evidence of his standing and prosperity. His household included two adopted children, one of them his brother Robert's, a chaplain and two servants. Rooms in the house almost certainly included a chapel in which was 'a great missale', a silver chalice with silver-gilt cover, silver cruets and a priest's chasuble of damask; a great hall hung with tapestries and lit with a brass candelabrum; and a best bedroom with feather beds and a double-bottomed chest for valuables. There were numerous silver pieces for his own use and pewter items for the kitchen.

Carpenter listed many personal bequests, some to nephews and nieces, some to friends, some to servants and their children, some to the priests of City churches. For the making of vessels for the churches of St Peter and St Martin he left 'fifty marks weight of my silver vessels which have very often served me for the unreasonable and vain glory of the world'. His fur gowns 'and other sumptuous vestments which, God forgive me, I have many times abused in superfluous and useless observances', he ordered to be sold and the proceeds used to buy useful clothing for poor and devout persons.

He also left money to a number of needy groups, including the poor lepers of Holborn, Locks and Hackney, the poor madmen of Bethlehem, and the poor prisoners of Newgate, Ludgate, the Fleet, Marshalsea and King's Bench. And he directed that any valuable books not named in other bequests should go to Guildhall Library – one of his duties as Whittington's executor had been to assist with the founding of this library. What John Carpenter's will does *not* include is any bequest to support and educate boys of the City of London.

It does, however, mention 'another will made of my lands and tenements' under which his wife would inherit twenty librates of land and rent. This will has never been found and it may or may not have included the lands and tenements which ultimately endowed his charity. All that is certain is that he either left these properties or gave them in his lifetime to two trusted friends, and that when the second friend died he in turn passed them on to John Don, a man of standing in the City, together with instructions about Carpenter's intentions for them.

John Don duly incorporated Carpenter's bequest in his own will, made out in 1477, 35 years after Carpenter's death, passing on Carpenter's properties to the

Guildhall Chapel, where 'Carpenter's Children' were to assist at divine service in the choir on festival days.

11

John Don's will.

Mayor, Chamberlain and Corporation of the City of London, together with Carpenter's instructions for the charity they were to support. This roundabout way of doing things had a purpose; Carpenter was afraid that if he left the properties to the Corporation he might offend against the statutes of alienation and mortmain, with the result that they would subsequently be confiscated. Don seems not to have had this anxiety.

In Carpenter's words, as John Don transferred them to his own will, Carpenter required the Mayor and Corporation to 'find and maintain . . . in perpetuity, four boys born within the City of London, who shall be called . . . "Carpenter's Children" to assist at divine service in the choir of the chapel of Guildhall on festival days' (which would include Sundays). On other days the boys were to study at schools most convenient for them. They were to be boarders and to 'eat, drink and live within the college of the said chapel or in another place near by'. They were to be given gowns, tunics, hose, shoes and shirts at a cost of 13*s.* 4*d.* a year each, and bedding, hair cutting and laundry at 26*s.* 8*d.* a year each. One of them was to attend, morning and evening, on the warden of the chapel if the warden wished it, as long as this did not interfere with his schooling. A tutor was to be provided for the four of them and paid 13*s.* 4*d.* a year. Only after these and a few other expenses had been met was the surplus to be used for the upkeep of the tenements.

Carpenter seems thus to have had two aims, but which was more important to him it is hard to say. Attached to Guildhall Chapel, which, like its library, he had helped to found, there was, according to John Stow in his *Survey of London,* 1598, a 'custos' or college, consisting of seven chaplains and three clerks. Carpenter apparently intended to add four choirboys to this establishment. On the other hand he also obviously wanted to give these City of London boys a good education. And, as well as his extensive library, his friends strongly suggest an interest in education. Among them were his namesake, Dr John Carpenter, Chancellor of Oxford, founder of S. Anthony's School where Sir Thomas More was a pupil; Master William Byngham, founder of a college for teachers at Cambridge; Sir John Neel who can be called founder of the Mercers' School; and Master William Lichfield, who a few years after Carpenter's death was one of those (along with Neel) who petitioned Parliament for the better regulation of grammar schools.

For 70 years Carpenter's children were almost certainly the choirboys of Guildhall Chapel which Carpenter had intended them to be, and got the education he wanted them to have. Who they were, what they were taught and exactly where they lived can only be guessed, indeed, it is only in 1536–7 that there is any certain evidence that they existed at all. Then, however, the earliest surviving City accounts record payments to one Mr Church of 3*s.* 4*d.* as 'tutor to the Children' and of 21*s.* 2*d.* for 'the cost of the children'. Mr Church was the Revd John Church, priest of Guildhall Library.

Eleven years later (1547) under the Chantries Act Guildhall Chapel and Library were forfeited and its books dispersed.

2

Children Without a Home

1547~1837

CARPENTER'S CHILDREN WERE also dispersed, either in 1547 or soon afterwards, but the bequest for their support remained and the City Corporation continued to use it for something akin to its original purpose. The next surviving City accounts (1563) include 'skole hyre' as one of the items in 'the accounts . . . for the landes of Mr John Carpenter'. These lands had brought in £27 3s. 3d. of which 10s. had been paid for overseeing the '4 children being poore men's children at schole and lernynge', £3 12s. for 'barbor, Lawnder, schole hyre and other necessaryes', £9 2s. for their food and £4 7s. for their clothes.

For almost 300 years (until the 1820s) the accounts continue to give details of the way in which the Carpenter bequest was spent for the children's benefit. Important items were two new coats a year for each child, one at Christmas, one at Whitsun. Each batch of four coats required about 5½ yards either of russet, a

Entries in the City of London cash accounts for the year 1633, showing disbursements of John Carpenter's bequest.

coarse, homespun, reddish-brown or grey cloth at 10s. a yard, or of the less expensive broadcloth, a black, plain-wove, dressed cloth at 7s. 6d. a yard, as well as 12 yards of cotton for lining at 8d. a yard. In 1584 James Harman, a yeoman of the chamber, was paid 10s. 4d. for making the eight coats and providing buttons.

Other payments besides those mentioned in 1563 were sometimes for shoes or hose and the Chamberlain paid himself an amount which eventually became 30s. a year for overseeing the children, suggesting that he took some special part in arranging their lives, but the sum spent in total on the children remained virtually the same, at £19 10s. a year. Since the purchasing power of money had greatly diminished by the end of the period the children were in reality receiving a much smaller benefit.

The accounts almost always describe them as poor (though Don's will does not use this word). And from 1692 onwards they are additionally described as freemen's children. But in one account book alone are a few of them named, and there is never any other indication of what sort of boys they were. Nor do the accounts give any idea where they were being taught or maintained. Only during the last 60 years has this mystery become a little less mysterious as a result of a detailed study of another set of documents, the City Acquittance Books.

In these books either the parents or the children themselves signed for their benefits, making it possible to bring the number known by name between 1649 and 1688 to 25, and (after a gap of almost 100 years when the Acquittance Books are missing, probably destroyed in the Guildhall fire of 1786) to discover a further 21 children between 1786 and the 1820s. Though no doubt poor by some standards, they do not seem to have come from what would now be called the working classes. One was the son of a plumber, two others of clerks, another of a minister and another of a scrivener, while the mother of another, Elizabeth Price, was the widow of a barber surgeon. Her entry reads:

> Received the 30th day of September 1660 by me Elizabeth Price of London, widow . . . the some of nineteen shillings towards the maintenance of my sonne Edward Price, viz., for his 3 months pension Ended at Michas. 1660 and for his commons for one quarter of a yeare ended at Michas. 1660, etc., and is by bequest of John Carpenter sometyme Towne Clerke of London, decd. I say received . . . 19s.

On the other hand some of them were apparently uneducated, able only to sign with their mark. Among these at first was William Scudamore (1820–7) but he eventually learned to sign competently.

Using the names from the Acquittance Books it became possible to search pupil lists of other London day schools to see if any of the 46 Carpenter's children appear there. None was found at St Paul's, but at Merchant Taylors' School Joseph Englebird is almost certainly the Carpenter's child Joseph Englebert (1663–5), and though three other Merchant Taylors' boys have less unusual names, making their identification less certain, Thomas Wells, Charles Williams and Edmund Archer were all probably Carpenter's children of the 1680s with the same names.

The third document to tell something about Carpenter's children in these years is the tenth report of the Charity Commission (1823). After giving details of the payments being made by the Chamberlain to himself and for the children it continues,

> The Chamberlain requires the parents from time to time to bring the copybooks of their children, and other specimens of their progress, to satisfy him of the proper application of the testator's bounty, and this has been the practice for many years back. Very little remains out of the respective shares of the persons benefited, after the object of education is satisfied, to be applied to clothing. The parents or friends of the children are required, quarterly, to give to the Chamberlain receipts for the payment of their children's education, which receipts are entered in the City's acquittance book.

It was the investigation by the Charities Commission of the Carpenter bequest which led to the most important change in the fortunes of Carpenter's children since the forfeiture of Guildhall Chapel in 1547, since it drew attention to the fact that, although the sum by which the children were benefiting had never changed, 'the rental of the Estate on which this bequest is charged' had 'very considerably increased'. Just what this income had become the Commission was not entirely sure since it was not certain which had been the Carpenter properties, but it 'understood' that they had been in Thames Street, Bridge Street, St Giles-in-the-Fields, Westcheap and Houndsditch, and identified properties 'answering or pretty nearly so' to those described in the 1633 account book. In 1826 these were producing an annual income of just over £750.

By the time the commissioners made their report the conscience of the Corporation had apparently been awakened, for it had told the Commission that it had taken 'great pains . . . by searching in the archives of the Corporation and other places for the will of John Carpenter, without effect'. It should, of course, have been looking for John Don's will. The purpose of the search was to discover what precisely the will required the Corporation to do. Some councilmen would have liked to find it in order to demonstrate that the Corporation was only bound to make specific payments for the children's education and support, and

The sole classroom at Tonbridge School until 1826, where the four Carpenter scholars were taught from 1827–1837.

was entitled to pocket the surplus, but most considered that this was unjust. As a result, in June 1826 the Council adopted a report from a select committee of the City Lands Committee (which had the responsibility for managing the Carpenter bequest) about what should be done instead.

During discussions leading up to this report various suggestions had been made which foresaw the future, most significantly that the bequest should be spent on the education of a greater number of boys, but for the moment its recommendation was a simple one: the four Carpenter scholars should be sent to Tonbridge Grammar School.

Though this was an improvement, and established the principle that the Corporation should give the children a much larger proportion of the bequest's income, not all the members of the Common Council were pleased. One, Richard Taylor, considered that at Tonbridge the boys would be 'brought up in a manner beyond their expectations and acquire habits inconsistent with their elevation in life'. Another suggested Christ's Hospital or Aldenham as alternative schools, but Christ's Hospital would not take them, and Aldenham (managed by the Brewers' Company) was considered too expensive, so it was to Tonbridge that they went.

Tonbridge may have been chosen because of its City connections. It had been established under the will of a benefactor, Sir Andrew Judd, in 1688 and since then managed by the Skinners' Company. In 1819 Judd's bequest had been investigated, as Carpenter's bequest was to be investigated, by the Charities Commission, which had drawn attention to the fact that, like Carpenter's bequest, it was earning far more than was being spent on the boys for whose benefit it had been intended, the Skinners' Company retaining the balance.

On the other hand, the school can hardly have seemed ideal. The City Corporation specifically required its four Carpenter scholars to be given a classical and commercial education, but the councilmen must have read what the Charities Commission had written about Tonbridge:

> The reason for the small number of foundation scholars . . . is probably the little importance attached by the inhabitants of Tonbridge to an education simply classical for their sons, compared with the benefits of a more general, commercial, or practical instruction, especially as the education so exclusively classical is not followed up by any considerable provision at College.

Since then, in 1825, Tonbridge had had new statutes, and these, far from encouraging a more commercial curriculum, had done the opposite by establishing 16 closed exhibitions to Oxford or Cambridge. When the head, Dr Thomas Knox, accepted the Carpenter scholars he asked that they should be allowed to stay until the age of 19 so that they could compete for these exhibitions. The Corporation's response (raising the leaving age of the scholars from 15 to only 16) suggests that although it had chosen Tonbridge it was still wanting something other than the standard middle-class Latin and Greek education for its scholars.

It would have liked to make their status even more apparent by having them dressed in 'Blue Jacket and Trowsers' and compelled to wear a small silver medal to show that they were 'the objects of the said charity', but about this Knox had his way, writing 'There should be no distinction, honorary or otherwise, at the School. All distinctions operate as an obstacle to improvement.' Nor would Knox agree that the Carpenter scholars, who were necessarily boarders, should have to spend their holidays at the school.

Just the same the seven Carpenter scholars who went from the City of London to Tonbridge School between 1827 and 1837 must have found the experience bewildering, particularly since some of them seem to have been academically entirely unqualified. About one, Knox wrote in 1827 that he could neither read nor write. Next year he told the Corporation, 'A Boy . . . has been sent by the present Lord Mayor – totally unfit to enter the School – his manners low and vulgar – his ignorance extreme – his faculties, I suspect imperfect. It is extraordinary that out of four boys two should be silly . . . with the exception of Scott I consider all the other boys a disgrace to the School.'

Under Dr Knox's influence (appropriately for a Kent school) Tonbridge was devoted to cricket. One boy remembered that sometimes Knox would

Dr Thomas Knox, the Headmaster of Tonbridge School, refused to allow the Carpenter boys to wear special clothes or medals to show their status, on the grounds that 'all distinctions operate as an obstacle to improvement'.

> enter into the schoolroom about ten o'clock in the morning or four o'clock on fine afternoons, and having informed the boys that he was well satisfied with the work either of the fifth or sixth forms, take a new cricket ball from his capacious pocket, and throw it into the centre of the School, as a signal that it was a let-out or a holiday, and with a shout the boys would make for the door and rush out into the field for a game of cricket.

Punishment at the school was 'almost always corporal. The unheard of punishment of writing out 500 lines of Homer was once given by the Doctor, who caught a boy, *flagrante delicto*, riding his favourite heifer round the cricket field.' True, the Corporation insisted that the Carpenter scholars should be taught French (and refused to pay for dancing or fencing), but it must seem doubtful whether they learned much from the 'old French officer' whom the School provided.

In 1827 when the first Carpenter scholars arrived at Tonbridge its boys numbered 110, but they must also have been there during its decline 'to a low ebb', at the time of the Reform Bill agitation, when Dr Knox gave 'much offence to many' by a speech he made at the great meeting at Penenden Heath. The last three Carpenter scholars were also there during the great frost of 1835–6 when the boys took all their half holidays consecutively, on condition they had none for the rest of the term. As a result they skated day after day for a month on the Summer Hill lake. 'At the termination of the frost the arrangement was adhered to – but for three weeks only; the restriction was too much for masters and boys.'

When any of the Carpenter scholars became 16 and left the school the Corporation gave him the generous grant of £100 towards his 'advancement in life'. None, it seems, advanced far, because none distinguished himself; indeed almost nothing is known about their subsequent lives.

3

A School is Founded: the Corporation, the Workhouse and the Honey Market

1827~1837

T HE CORPORATION'S DECISION to send the Carpenter scholars to Tonbridge School by no means ended the debate about the bequest, if for no other reason than that this still only absorbed about £420 of the bequest's £750 income. Richard Taylor was one of two men who continued to urge the Common Council to use this income more properly. It was Taylor who, as well as criticising the choice of Tonbridge, had suggested that the bequest be used to educate a greater number of boys and for this purpose he now recommended 'promoting a day school in London'. The bequest might, he considered, be able to present 40 boys to a school of this sort.

In December 1828 Taylor, pursuing this suggestion, gave notice of a motion in Common Council asking for a report on how the earnings of the Carpenter bequest could best be used 'for the benefit of the largest possible number of sons of bona-fide freeman-householders of the City and none other'. Four and a half months later for unexplained reasons he withdrew the motion.

By trade Taylor was a printer. One partner in his firm was his nephew, J. E. Taylor, founder of the *Manchester Guardian*. But his interests were far wider, including Italian poetry, Teutonic dialects and above all natural history. He became Secretary of the Linnean Society and was editor of the periodical, *Annals and Magazine of Natural History*. In public life he was a member of the Court of Common Council for 35 years. But it was his interest in education which was to have the most lasting consequences. He and his brother John had already helped in the founding of University College, London, which obtained parliamentary approval in 1826 and was to open its school in 1830. And he was to be a Governor of the proposed City of London *Corporation* School.

This school (to be carefully distinguished from the City of London School) had its origins in the London Workhouse. Founded two years after the Restoration, the Workhouse had in part been a prison for 'vagrants and disorderly persons', but had

always had as one of its purposes the 'education and apprenticing of poor children'. By 1820, however, it had so deteriorated that the Common Council appointed a special committee to investigate it. The committee reported that the cause of the decay was the view taken by the Governors that their duties had become obsolete and unnecessary.

Nine years later (1829) the Corporation finally obtained an Act of Parliament allowing it to put into practice its solution to the problem: the full transformation of the Workhouse into a school. Like the Workhouse, this would be for 'the maintenance of poor and destitute children . . . and for apprenticing all or any such children to industrious trades'.

For its maintenance it would have the Workhouse's previous income of £300 a year. But from the start its Governors considered this insufficient and tried to obtain more support from the Corporation. To do so they began to alter their plans for their school and within two years were describing it as 'a school which might emphatically be termed the High School of the City of London'. Their formal prospectus issued in April 1832 retained the Act of Parliament's description, but on the same day Alderman Copeland submitted notes which pointed out their dilemma: that the school might either be for the education of the children of persons in reduced circumstances or for the children of the middle classes.

Five days later the Corporation made the school a grant of £2,000, but even this did not satisfy the Governors, who within a month had identified another source of support, and on 7 May submitted the following address to the Council:

Part of the London Workhouse, used 'for the relief and employment of the poor, the punishment of vagrants and disorderly persons, and apprenticing of poor children', and the adjoining Ludgate Prison, 1815. When the Workhouse was wound up in 1829, its income was to go 'towards the maintenance of a school for poor and destitute children'.

That even in very early times the Education of our future Citizens was deemed important is well supported by the Donation of John Carpenter, Town Clerk of this City in the reign of Henry the 5th, who left estates for the education of Children of Freemen of the City, and it is only to be regretted that this Charity which is possessed of so large an annual income derived from those estates is to be confined to the education of four boys only.

At a meeting the same month the school's Governors passed two apparently incompatible resolutions. While one declared that the school was to be for 'the maintenance, clothing, education and apprenticing of poor children', the other described its nature as 'what is commonly known by the name of a Grammar School'.

Meanwhile, throughout 1832 the City Lands Committee had been postponing the discussion of a question first raised that May: 'Whether any better mode can be adopted for promoting the object of the Carpenter Charity.' Eventually on 5 December it resolved that 'the present application of Carpenter's Charity is highly objectionable and ought to be more extensively useful', and appointed a deputation to communicate the resolution to the Lord Mayor.

Taylor was a member of this deputation, but, more significantly for the future, the City Lands Committee which had appointed it had recently been joined by the other man who was to campaign for a proper use of Carpenter's bequest, Warren Stormes Hale, often described as the City of London School's second founder.

Hale was by trade a candle-maker. At the age of 13 he had started work as an apprentice in his brother's wax-chandling business in Cannon Street. By 1832, aged 41, he had made a fortune, using French chemists' discoveries about animal and vegetable fats, but he never hid his humble background. Years later (1883) the Old Boy, Henry Fagan (CLS 1840–6) wrote about him, 'Only a tallow chandler,

Part of John Ogilby's Map of the City of London, showing the site of Honey Lane Market (centre), on which the first City of London School was built. Guildhall, where the first Carpenter's Children were educated, is barely a block away (above right).

not like the City Men who now live at Brighton, Croydon, or Surbiton, but one who had lived and worked amongst his men, and was not ashamed that everybody should know it. I fear the snobbishness of boys did not fully see the man behind the tallow; but still we did like and respect him.' By then Hale had died, having been Alderman, Sheriff and in 1864–5 Lord Mayor of London.

Now, in January 1833, he became Chairman of the City Lands Committee. Four months later this committee, and the Governors of the 'Corporation School' obtained the response for which they had been hoping when the Corporation ordered the City Lands Committee first to consider how to make the Carpenter bequest 'more extensively used', and second 'to consider consolidating it with the City of London Corporation School'. The Governors of the Corporation School and the City Lands Committee now began to co-operate, and selected as a site for the school, Honey Lane Market, a market place just north of Cheapside which had once been important but was now in decline. The Lands Committee meeting which took this decision, however, made a provision which was ultimately to prove fatal to unification. Its resolution read,

> That it is the opinion of this Committee that the site of Honey Lane Market should be granted for the purpose, provided an Act of Parliament is obtained to authorize the same, and such alterations are made in the arrangements as may secure to the Citizens of London a School for the education of Children on a more extensive scale and on the most liberal and improved principles, but not otherwise.

In other words the Lands Committee was saying again that it wanted a school of a kind for which the Corporation School's funds, derived as they were from the old Workhouse, could not properly be used. The surprising thing is that it was not until nine months later (July 1834) when the necessary parliamentary Bill had received its second reading in the House of Lords and reached its committee stage, that the problem was recognised. Then, on 26 July, the City Lands Committee was told by one of its members, Edward Tyrell, that a difficulty had been 'raised at the House of Lords with respect to the funds of the London Workhouse, and that the same could not be applied by the Bill before the House to the purposes of the proposed School – that he with Warren Stormes Hale, Esq., the Chairman of the Sub-Committee [of the City Lands Committee] had seen the Lord Chancellor and other noble Lords who concurred therein . . . and that he had altered the Bill accordingly.'

Altering the Bill was no small matter. From the original draft of 19 folio pages, nine or nearly half were now deleted – all those which made any reference to the 1829 Bill and the London Workhouse.

Winners by this arrangement were Hale and his supporters on the City Lands Committee, for they got the sort of school they wanted, together with an annual £900 from the Carpenter bequest (the amount it was earning) and the Honey Lane Market as a site. Losers were the Governors of the Corporation School who were left with no site and did not find one for another 20 years. However, they retained the old Workhouse income, together with the subsequent £2,000 grant from the Corporation, and neither the Corporation nor Hale abandoned them. Hale became their chairman and eventually in 1854, largely as a result of his efforts, they

Lord Henry Brougham, Lord Chancellor, who was one of those responsible for the fate of the proposed City of London School.

First page of the Act to establish the City of London School.

opened their school at Brixton as the Freemens' Orphanage School. Today it flourishes as the City of London Freemens' School at Ashtead, Surrey.

On the House of Lords Committee which 'altered' the 1834 Bill were two prominent radical politicians of the time, Lord Shaftesbury, remembered for his social reform Bills, particularly the Factory Act of 1833 which among other things forbade the employment of children under nine in factories; and Lord Brougham, inventor of the famous four-wheel carriage, Lord Chancellor under Prime Ministers Grey and Melbourne, passionate supporter of the Great Reform Bill of 1832. Brougham gave personal advice on the revision of the Honey Lane Market Bill, as it was called, and on 29 July, just three days after its defects had been noticed, Lord Shaftesbury presented the revised Bill to the House of Lords for its third reading.

This Act, apart from listing the 119 houses from which the Carpenter bequest drew its income, was a comparatively simple affair of 20 clauses. Essentially it gave the 'Mayor, Aldermen and Commons of the City of London' the duty to maintain a school on the site of the Honey Lane Market, in place of Carpenter's Charity.

The Act left to the Corporation almost every other decision about the sort of school it should be and the way it should be run, but it did include a few requirements. The School was to be 'for the religious and virtuous Education of Boys, and for instructing them in the higher Branches of Literature and all other useful Learning'. And it was to use and teach the authorised version of the Bible and to read prayers every morning and evening.

It also empowered the Corporation to appoint 'one or more committees' to manage the School, an important permission since it led to the establishment of the City of London School Committee. For 33 years Hale was Chairman of this

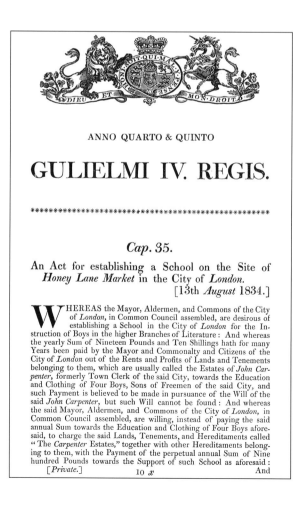

ANNO QUARTO & QUINTO

GULIELMI IV. REGIS.

****

Cap. 35.

An Act for establishing a School on the Site of *Honey Lane Market* in the City of *London*.
[13th *August* 1834.]

WHEREAS the Mayor, Aldermen, and Commons of the City of *London*, in Common Council assembled, are desirous of establishing a School in the City of *London* for the Instruction of Boys in the higher Branches of Literature: And whereas the yearly Sum of Nineteen Pounds and Ten Shillings hath for many Years been paid by the Mayor and Commonalty and Citizens of the City of *London* out of the Rents and Profits of Lands and Tenements belonging to them, which are usually called the Estates of *John Carpenter*, formerly Town Clerk of the said City, towards the Education and Clothing of Four Boys, Sons of Freemen of the said City, and such Payment is believed to be made in pursuance of the Will of the said *John Carpenter*, but such Will cannot be found: And whereas the said Mayor, Aldermen, and Commons of the City of *London*, in Common Council assembled, are willing, instead of paying the said annual Sum towards the Education and Clothing of Four Boys aforesaid, to charge the said Lands, Tenements, and Hereditaments called "The *Carpenter* Estates," together with other Hereditaments belonging to them, with the Payment of the perpetual annual Sum of Nine hundred Pounds towards the Support of such School as aforesaid:
[*Private.*]   10 *x*   And

committee, and he must be credited with much of what it achieved for the School. The creation of this committee gave the School two tiers of management. The School Committee was in many ways the equivalent of the Boards of Governors which other schools had, but whereas these were fully responsible for the finances and management of their schools, the powers of the City of London School Committee were limited in so far as the Common Council of the Corporation reserved important ones for itself.

A minor difference soon occurred. When a subcommittee of the School Committee sent its proposals for the regulation of the school to the Common Council, the Common Council rejected the suggestion that the Carpenter scholars should remain at Tonbridge until they were 16, and instead they were duly transferred to the new school as soon as it opened.

The School's most urgent need was a building. From 41 plans submitted to a competition, those of J. B. Bunning, future City Architect, were chosen. They proposed a fine-looking building in neo-Gothic style, with an imposing entrance, to become known as Lord Mayor's Entrance, from Milk Street, below battlements and turrets suggesting a medieval castle. What old prints fail to show is that it was almost unbelievably small. It would have occupied just half of today's School playground.

Inside, at the opposite (east) end from the Milk Street entrance was the building's most striking feature, the so-called Theatre, a lecture hall similar to the Royal Institution's lecture theatre in Albemarle Street, built in 1799–1801, the lecturer performing on basement level, his audience surrounding him on row above row of steeply tiered seats. The rest of the ground floor provided the Headmaster's study, a library and sundry classrooms. There were more classrooms on the first floor, while in the south-west corner on three floors the Headmaster was to have his accommodation. Below, in the basement were kitchen, lunch room, tuckshop, wine and beer cellar, privies, 'washing troughs', and that best-remembered of all features, the horseshoe. This was a seven-foot wide passage of horseshoe shape forming an almost complete circle below the tiered seats of the Theatre. When the Common Council considered Bunning's plan it asked for the inclusion of 'suitable accommodation for the pupils in the intervals between the hours of study', but Bunning said that this would be impossible without 'material alterations', so it was the horseshoe which became the School's playground.

Plans for laying the foundation stone led to a more dramatic confrontation when the School Committee, after failing to get the Duke of Sussex, asked Lord Brougham to perform the ceremony. Hearing of this, the Lord Mayor (who considered that he should have been invited) asked the Committee 'by what authority such an arrangement was made . . . to which he certainly cannot consent'.

The School Committee replied that it acted under authority of the clause of the 1834 Act which authorised the Common Council to set up committees to manage the School. At this the Lord Mayor threatened to write to Brougham to forbid him to come into the City; and on the eve of the occasion told a deputation from the School Committee that he would have Brougham taken into custody if he attempted to perform the ceremony. The School Committee responded by telling its architect, builder and their employees to take orders from the Committee's

WINCHESTER *VERSUS* BROUGHAM, OR A RUMPUS OVER THE FIRST STONE OF THE CITY OF LONDON SCHOOL!

THE RIVAL STONE MASONS,

Or a Flare-up between Winchester and Brougham, about Laying the First Stone of the new Cockney School!

Winchester. I say you have no right whatsoever to poke your lanthorn jaws into the city, you itinerant vagabond! Is it fair, I ax of any one, that you have a right to monopolize the building of all the knowledge shops and Poor Law workhouses, to the exclusion of every body else, you dry bread and water-gruel looking warmint?— Come on, if you are a man!

Two contemporary pictures depicting the laying of the foundation stone of the City of London School.

chairman only, and the Lord Mayor apparently submitted, for on 21 July 1835 Brougham duly laid the stone.

The tender accepted for the new School was £11,320, a sum paid by the Corporation, so compensating for the profits it had made over nearly three centuries from Carpenter's bequest. And the Corporation continued to support the School, giving it an important advantage over many London schools (King's College School, for example) with no endowment and no similar backer.

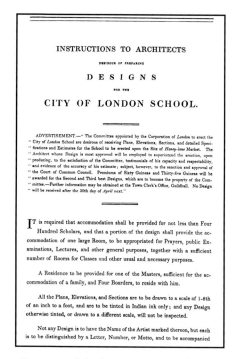

First page of the 'Instructions to architects desirous of preparing designs for the City of London School'.

4

The Problems of
Headmaster Giles

1837~1840

THE NEW CITY OF LONDON SCHOOL also needed a Headmaster, and the 1834 Act was strangely precise about the way he and his deputy, whom it called the First and Second Masters, should be chosen. All candidates for these positions were to be examined by six professors, those of divinity, classics and mathematics from King's College, London, and those of Greek, mathematics and natural philosophy (science) from the University of London (University College). Interestingly, the unamended Bill had named the King's professor of natural and experimental philosophy instead of divinity, suggesting the sort of school which Hale and the original drafters had wanted. These six professors were to choose the three best candidates for each position, from whom the Common Council was to make its final selection.

The clause demonstrates that the foundation of the City of London School was not an isolated event, but part of a general burgeoning of English education between the end of the Napoleonic Wars in 1815 and the middle of the century. In this great expansion and reformation the boarding public schools as they were now being called, came second. True there were the seven so-called Great Schools, and Thomas Arnold arrived at one of these, Rugby, in 1828, but he was little heard about until the late 1830s and his achievements were for many years afterwards misunderstood. Though he civilised (or, as he would have put it, re-Christianised) Rugby, he never promoted games, his reforms of the almost exclusively Greek and Latin curriculum were minimal and his use of the Sixth Form to rule the school was only seen with hindsight to have been intended to produce District Officers to manage the empire. Even when, from 1841 onwards, Cheltenham, Marlborough, Rossall, Radley, Lancing, Bradfield and a dozen other new boarding schools opened, they also at first taught little besides the classics.

London was far ahead, both in the founding of new colleges and schools, and in introducing the teaching of modern subjects, as a result of the efforts of half a dozen radical politicians and educationalists. Besides Brougham, these included Bentham, the Utilitarian philosopher, who had proposed a school for the middle

Revd John Allen Giles, Headmaster 1837–40.

classes in 1815, Francis Place 'the radical tailor', and George Birkbeck, founder in 1826 of Birkbeck College, first called the London Mechanics Institute, with its lectures, museum and chemical laboratory. The same year came the founding of University College, London, which began its lectures in Gower Street in 1828 and opened its school in 1830. The following year, as a direct Church-of-England response to the non-sectarian University College, King's College opened in the Strand with a school in its basement.

When eventually after much difficulty four of the six professors named in the 1834 Act managed to assemble in one place they considered seven applicants for First Master of the City of London School and duly short listed three, one of them Mr Brewer, presumably the recently elected School secretary. The Common Council, however, chose the Revd John Allen Giles. Giles was 29, had won a double first at Corpus Christi College, Oxford, and for the last four years been head of Camberwell Collegiate School. He was appointed on 24 November 1836 and the School was officially opened just over two months later on 2 February 1837, Hale's birthday.

At 9.25 a.m. that morning the porter opened the front (Milk Street) doors and a crush of boys pushed in. Several later claimed to have been first. In 1887 William Berry (1837–42), who had emigrated to New Zealand, presented the John Carpenter Club with a silver punch bowl inscribed with his claim. Five years later Archdeacon William Emery (1837–43) told Old Boys that he had been first, along with Robert Warwick (1837–43), whom he was protecting and took in beside him. But two other boys, Thomas Williams (1837–9) and Charles Hutton (1837) claimed to have been allowed in earlier by the side (Honey Lane Market) door; and the truth seems to be that Hale's son Joseph was let in still earlier through the Milk Street door by Hale himself, half an hour before it was officially opened.

By 3 p.m. the boys were assembled in the upper rows of the Theatre, each with a bun and a glass of wine, ready to be addressed by the important visitors. These included the Lord Mayor (Alderman Kelly), several other members of the Common Council, Dr Birkbeck and, significantly, William Richie, Professor of Natural Philosophy at University College, London – one of those who had short-listed the Headmaster. 'The spectacle was . . . the most animated imaginable,' the *Morning Chronicle* reported, 'and the most intense delight was manifested during the whole of the proceedings.' The Mayor told the story of the Carpenter bequest, then Professor Richie spoke. 'We had a grand lecture by Professor Richie; I cannot remember a word of it, but I know it was interesting' (Emery). In fact Richie made the sort of comments on current educational practice to be expected from a science professor, criticising the typical classics curriculum of the day. On the other hand, his suggestion for easing boys from one discipline to the other consisted of 'showing in what manner the reading of Ovid and other Latin authors could be made to combine with the study of sciences with which such authors displayed an acquaintance'. Nor was he tactful about the teaching profession, observing that 'many entered upon this most difficult of all business without being possessed of any qualifications whatever, and the schoolmaster's profession seemed to be a sort of refuge when men failed in all others'.

He was addressing 200 boys, to increase by the following month to 495 (95 more than the School building had been designed to accommodate) – evidence

Opposite page: *The first City of London School, Milk Street, drawn by Hablot Brown after a sketch by R. Garland.*

One of the original 200 boys at the school in 1837, T. J. Nelson went on to gain a knighthood and become Solicitor to the City of London.

Thomas Hall, one of the first masters, who was later to become the School's first science master.

that middle-class demand in London for reputable day schools had not been satisfied by the schools of King's College and University College, though these, too, had shown dramatic early growth, King's from 85 to 350 by 1834, University College from 58 to 249 by 1833. Almost all who came to the City of London School were day boys apart from the Carpenter scholars who boarded at the School with Dr Giles; most lived close enough to walk to school since their fathers were either City freemen or householders. The annual fee these parents paid was £8 – modest compared to King's (18 guineas) and University College's (£15).

To teach those 200 boys there was, of course, Giles – in the tradition of the time the Sixth Form's classics master. Below him came the Second Master, Robert Edkins, chosen with the help of the same professors who had made their short list of three from 14 applicants. Edkins, a mathematician, established the tradition that the senior mathematics master was also the Fifth Form master. While no boys remembered Giles as a teacher, many remembered Edkins. Nicknamed 'Skins', he was short-tempered and a hopeless disciplinarian. He was also short-sighted. Boys would chalk white squares on the floor and 'much rejoice when told to "pick up that piece of paper".' This they would try in vain to do until, 'worn out with waiting, he dashed down to the place only to find how he had been swindled'. Or they would scatter about the floor devices known as skip-jacks, made from walnut shells, rubber bands, match sticks and cobbler's wax, which would 'go off one after another with a loud "plop" till poor Mr Edkins' temper was frayed to pieces'.

As punishments Edkins would set impossible impositions, for example 'a whole book of Euclid, to be written out in a single evening'. Edwin Abbott (1850–7, the future Headmaster), writing about his own religious development and trying to distinguish between immoral and venial actions, remembered that he and his fellow pupils would consider cheating in an exam immoral but cheating in class merely venial. Furthermore, 'to cheat our mathematical master (who was eccentric to the verge of madness) was thought not only venial but even necessary'.

Alternatively Edkins would expel boys from his class, who then had 'the pleasure of rambling about the School for a day or two during the mathematical hours as a punishment'. In 1846 the Headmaster reported to the School Committee that one boy had had no mathematical lessons for five weeks. On the other hand, H. S. Fagan (1840–6, later Head of Bath Grammar School) claimed that Edkins turned out 'more single-figure wranglers than any other master of his day'. Certainly the first three scholarships won by boys, all to Cambridge, were for mathematics. And out of the classroom 'it was difficult to believe that we were dealing with the same man'. After he had left, William Huggins (1837–9) remembered how he had been pressed by Edkins to come to him for help 'in any mathematical difficulty' he might have. Huggins became one of the greatest modern astronomers; it was his inspiration to use the spectroscope to investigate heavenly bodies, so establishing that the nebulae were gaseous, not star clusters as previously thought.

In addition there were at least eight other masters, these all appointed by the School Committee at a meeting held 19 days before the School opened. They included a writing master, H. Manley, who had walked from Somerset to apply for the job, his assistant, Thomas Hall, to become the first science master, a drawing master, J. W. Allen, a German and Hebrew master, C. C. H. Bialloblotzky, and a French master, C. J. Delille, the author of well-regarded textbooks.

It was Delille whom Giles told on that first morning to 'sort those boys'. Delille did so by arranging them in order of height. As a result clever boys who were small were put into low classes. Emery, short for his age, went into the lowest, was promoted after three days into the Sixth, then after two weeks demoted into the Fifth.

By then Giles had given at least some of them a simple examination in groups of 20. The only question Huggins remembered being asked was to put into Latin, 'I love my mother'. Because he got it right he was made top of his group. Under Giles the classics were undoubtedly still considered the school's most important subject. Some of the newly founded schools were just as conservative. The first headmaster of University College School wrote, 'It is distinctly proposed that the School shall not be designed for the instruction of pupils in science.' Knox at Tonbridge had been typical of the heads of older schools in considering it not his duty to teach anything but the classics.

On the other hand the regulations of the City of London School, as approved by the Common Council on 23 September 1836, began their list of subjects to be taught to the whole school with reading aloud, English grammar and composition. Latin and Greek followed, but French, mathematics, natural philosophy and 'lectures on Chemistry and other branches of Experimental Philosophy' were also included and Hebrew could be learned free by any boy whose parent wished it, while German, Italian, Spanish and drawing were available for 'a moderate extra charge'.

This modern curriculum might seem the more remarkable for having been drawn up with the advice of the Headmasters of King's College School and University College School, Dr Major and Professor Malden, for both were classicists. Major was the compiler of the best-known Greek lexicon, before it was supplanted by Liddell and Scott's in 1843, and Malden, though the successor of the Headmaster who had rejected science for his school, was nevertheless also the Professor of Greek at the College. Major on the other hand had wider interests. In 1856 he was to become the founder secretary of the London Photographic Society, he would attend science lectures at his school, and his first prospectus for King's included German, Spanish, Italian, natural philosophy and 'the other branches of knowledge and science'.

Prospectuses, however, were one thing, practice another, and whatever advice Major may have given, nothing scientific was taught at King's until 1855. To take another example, Marlborough's proposed prospectus (1842) included Hebrew, French, German, drawing and experimental philosophy, but its teaching included no science until 1871. The question to ask is not what was promised but what was actually taught.

There is little doubt that the City of London School was ahead, probably the most advanced of all English schools, in the teaching of science. On 7 February 1838 the Revd William Cook, appointed assistant classics and mathematical master the previous month, was provided by the Committee with an air pump, glass tubes, a condensing syringe, a small quantity of mercury and a lathe 'for constructing any necessary appendages, together with a room in which to store them'. Though Cook left in November he offered to return if wanted to deliver occasional science lectures as he felt sure that they were 'highly useful to the pupils and creditable to the School generally (to which he felt a strong attachment)'.

14 YOUNG'S ELEMENTS OF EUCLID,

PROP. IV. THEOREM.

If two triangles have two sides of the one equal to two sides of the other, each to each; and have likewise the angles contained by those sides equal to one another; they shall likewise have their bases, or third sides, equal, and the two triangles shall be equal; and their other angles shall be equal, each to each, viz. those to which the equal sides are opposite.

Let ABC, DEF be two triangles, which have the two sides AB, AC, equal to the two sides DE, DF, each to each, viz. AB to DE, and AC to DF; and the angle BAC equal to the angle EDF; the base BC shall be equal to the base EF; and the triangle ABC to the triangle DEF; and the other angles to which the equal sides are opposite, shall be equal, each to each, viz. the angle ABC to the angle DEF, and the angle ACB to DFE.

For, if the triangle ABC be applied to DEF, so that the point A may be on D, and the straight line AB upon DE; the point B shall coincide with the point E, because AB is equal† to DE: and AB coinciding with DE, AC shall fall upon DF, because the angle BAC is equal† to the angle EDF; wherefore also the point C shall coincide with the point F, because the straight line AC† is equal to DF: but the point B was proved to coincide with the point E; wherefore the base BC shall coincide with the base EF: because, the point B coinciding with E, and C with F, if the base BC did not coincide with the base EF, two straight lines would enclose a space, which is impossible * Therefore the base BC coincides with the base EF, and therefore is equal to it. Wherefore the whole triangle ABC coincides with the whole triangle DEF, and is equal to it; and the other angles of the one coincide with the remaining angles of the other, and are equal to them, viz. the angle ABC to the angle DEF, and the angle ACB to

BOOK I. PROP. V. 15

DFE. Therefore, if two triangles have two sides of the one equal to two sides of the other, each to each, and have likewise the angles contained by those sides equal to one another, their bases shall likewise be equal, and the triangles shall be equal, and their other angles to which the equal sides are opposite shall be equal, each to each. Which was to be demonstrated.

PROP. V. THEOR.

The angles at the base of an isosceles triangle are equal to one another; and if the equal sides be produced, the angles upon the other side of the base shall be equal.

Let ABC be an isosceles triangle, of which the side AB is equal to AC, and let the straight lines AB, AC be produced to D and E: the angle CBD shall be equal to the angle BCE.

In BD take any point F, and from AE the greater, cut off AG equal* to AF the less, and join FC, GB. Because AF is equal to† AG, and AB to† AC, the two sides FA, AC are equal to the two GA, AB, each to each; and they contain the angle at A common to the two triangles AFC, AGB; therefore the base FC is equal* to the base GB, and the triangle AFC, to the triangle AGB, and the remaining angles of the one are equal* to the remaining angles of the other, each to each, to which the equal sides are opposite; viz. the angle ACF to the angle ABG, and the angle AFC to the angle AGB: and because the whole AF is equal to the whole AG, of which the parts AB, AC, are equal; the remainder BF is equal* to the remainder CG; and FC was proved to be equal to GB; therefore the two sides BF, FC are equal to the two CG, GB, each to each; and the angle BFC was proved to be equal to the angle CGB, wherefore the two triangles BFC, CGB; are equal*, and their remaining angles each to each, to which the equal sides are opposite: therefore the angle FBC is equal to the angle GCB, and the angle BCF

Pages from an edition of Euclid, 1840, used by boys at the School, including the 'pons asinorum'.

29

William Huggins, the astronomer, was one of many taught mathematics by Robert Edkins, the Second Master.

The School was also unusual in appointing foreigners to teach foreign languages. As late as 1890 Bell at Marlborough told a journalist, 'I so much believe in discipline I have no foreign masters . . . . All our French and German is taught . . . by Englishmen.' Bell was protecting himself against the sort of French teaching which went on at Highgate School where in the 1840s 'A snuff-taking old French gentleman came once a week, and sat at the end of the table, while a dozen boys fought round it, larked, and shot paper pellets into his frizzy hair.'

At the City of London School there were also problems. Those of Dr Bialloblotzky began early when, in August 1837, Giles told the School Committee that 'the German and Hebrew classes . . . are in a very unsatisfactory state – there is a great want of discipline and good order in them . . . the boys appear to be making little or no progress in these departments'. Bialloblotzky replied with many complaints (often, for example, he had to share a classroom with another master's class) and the Committee devised a list of regulations to assist him. For a time all went well, and the external examiner gave the German class a good report at midsummer 1838 and a fair one at midsummer 1839. In September 1839, however, Giles wrote again to the Committee, 'I cannot refrain from once more calling the attention of the committee to the German class. I am convinced that nothing is learnt, and what is worse the state of things therein causes great disorder throughout the school.'

The School Committee now appointed a special committee with Hale as its chairman to investigate the School in general, and on 18 December this produced a 45-page report on the German class alone. Its conclusions were an almost total vindication of Bialloblotzky. The root of the problem was that German classes took place at the same times as classes in regular subjects, causing great annoyance to Giles and Edkins when many of their boys would be missing. But Giles, the Committee noted, had admitted that he could have solved this problem, and he had failed to do so. It was the Headmaster's duty, the report concluded, 'with regard to every appointed Study, whatever may be his own views as to its importance, rather to extend to it his protection and countenance, than either to deprecate, or suffer, much less occasion, obstacles to its successful prosecution'.

In Giles's defence it must be admitted that Bialloblotzky taught in broken English and was paranoid. Fagan remembered that he was 'at loggerheads with the Committee, and every now and again would take a wild dislike to a boy whom he would accuse of being "von shpy", employed to report on his teaching'. Exonerated Bialloblotzky may have been, but he left the following year.

Delille had the advantage that French was a regular rather than an extra subject. Furthermore Fagan remembered him to have been an exceptional teacher.

> The number of classes he had at various institutions was marvellous. To us it seemed as if he was always either holding a class or correcting proofs, except at those delightful evenings at home to which we elder boys were at rare intervals invited, and at which . . . the host would be persuaded to sit down at the piano and give us
>
> 'Ah, qu'il est beau, qu'il est beau, qu'il est beau,
> Le post-ill-on, de Long-ju-u-u-u-meau.'

I owe a great deal to Delille – he taught me the use of my voice – he was recitation master and prompter at our theatrical scenes: and what a delight it was to be allowed to go now and then and see him act in something out of the *Bourgeois Gentilhomme*, or the *Plaideurs*, at one of his young men's classes.

Delille was also a disciplinarian, and a complaint he made to the School Committee on 12 September 1839 was another of the reasons for its appointment of the Special Committee to inquire into the state of the School. One of Delille's boys had refused to write a detention for him. When told that he would be kept after school until it had been written, the boy had 'coolly . . . said "I am accustomed to dine late".' Delille had appealed to Giles but Giles had 'invited me to relax my endeavours' and it was only next day when the boy heard that Delille had written to the School Committee that he had complied.

The third and equally important reason for the appointment of the Special Committee was a fall in the School's numbers. Giles had been asked to comment on this and had made two significant suggestions: that one way to remedy the decline might be to start a commercial class for boys going into business; and that another might be to abolish the rule which restricted boys to the sons of freemen or householders; he had been told that 30 or 40 suitable boys had recently been rejected for this reason. But the School Committee would not agree to recommend either remedy.

The Special Committee carried out its inquiry in October and November (alongside its inquiry into the German class), submitting its report which also ran to some 45 pages on 4 December. In this it gave details of interviews it had held with the School's masters. Their most general complaint about the Headmaster was that he rarely visited their classes or gave them advice, and that they did not trust him to support them in maintaining discipline.

The report was given to Giles and he was asked to reply in writing, but this he at first refused to do, asking instead to be interviewed by the Committee in the presence of a friend, then appealing to the 'Grand [School] Committee'. He had some grounds for distrusting the Special Committee, since he had never been told that it was interviewing his staff, but comments he now made suggest that he may also have been suffering from persecution delusions. 'I believe that a secret influence has been employed in the Special Committee against me,' he said. 'There are at least two or three facts stated in the report which could not have come to the knowledge of the Special Committee had they not been provided by members of that Special Committee.' Whether or not he was right in his suspicions, he was not allowed to appeal to the Grand Committee and next day (19 December) submitted the written answer to the Special Committee's report which it had asked for. He was subsequently allowed to cross-examine some of the masters who had been interviewed, but neither his letter nor his cross-examinations convinced the Special Committee and finally on 8 January the School Committee asked him to resign. By this time it was with discipline in the School and the trust other masters had in Giles that it was entirely concerned, and Delille's comment suggests that it probably reached the correct conclusion. 'A concentrated power is wanted in the School whose frown would be a punishment and whose smile a reward.'

On the other hand Giles's position had never been an easy one. He was required to consult the School Committee before he could take the smallest decision. For example, in September 1838 he needed to write to it:

> I beg leave to call your attention to an important subject. Many of the boys have lost umbrellas or have taken away old ones instead of good ones which they had brought with them. Repeated complaints have been made, some of them in an angry tone. The evil is without remedy so long as all the classes are allowed to put their umbrellas together in the same place . . . . The porter at this moment has in his possession 48 old umbrellas! I beg to suggest the propriety of dividing the umbrella stand into 3 or 4 parts and placing them so that each may stand near the door of one or more of the classrooms.

His ideas for the School's development were imaginative and sometimes ahead of their time. He claimed personal responsibility for a proposal two months before it opened that pupils in higher classes should be placed in three subdivisions to specialise in (a) the classics, (b) science and mathematics, or (c) modern languages and bookkeeping, according to the 'standing in life' which they planned to fill. This was to suggest the sort of modern side which was first formed at King's College School in 1850, but not at most public schools until many years later.

In September 1839 he begged to remind the School Committee 'that they have never yet considered the subject of Scientific Lectures in the Theatre' (William Cook's lectures of a year and a half earlier had apparently been forgotten). A month later Giles proposed a reversal of what had happened at King's College and University College: that the City of London School should develop a 'Senior Department as a college'. Such a college could become part of the new University of London, to the School's great benefit. The Committee considered this beyond its remit, and took no action.

Thirteen years after Giles's resignation he was sentenced to a year in prison for marrying a couple out of hours and doctoring his parish's records, but again his intentions (to protect the bride from parish curiosity) seem to have been good, and after three months he was released by royal warrant. He lived until 1884, teaching privately, publishing about 200 books (including 'Dr Giles's Juvenile Library'), and for his last 17 years holding the living of Sutton in Surrey.

5

Mortimer Gives Style

1840~1865

THE SCHOOL COMMITTEE, anxious no doubt to avoid another mistake, chose a slightly older man to succeed Giles. The Revd George Mortimer, 35, had other qualifications: at Oxford (Queen's and Balliol) he had won a double first in Greats, two years later he had become headmaster of Newcastle Grammar School, and for the last seven years had been head of Brompton Proprietary School. He also had presence (he was 'a tall, handsome, stately man') and a private income, enabling him to accept the modest salary of £500 plus £1 for every boy over 400. Many years later he said 'I have always been in the position that I have a very comfortable independent fortune of my own, and for the last 17 years I have remained at the School merely because I thought I was useful there.' The Committee's choice was to prove an excellent one.

The speech which Mortimer delivered in the Theatre on his introduction to the boys was described by Emery, now in the Sixth Form, as 'genial, fatherly and practical'. In more than one sense Mortimer was fatherly. He had a total of 16 children, ten of whom went to the School; one was born there (before he moved out to make space for extra classrooms) and another died there. He also took a paternal interest in the other boys and was said to know them all individually. 'His talk was always of boys,' Fagan remembered, ' – what some had done, what others were likely to do – and when years after I used to go and dine with him, he was always talking of boys of whom of course I knew little or nothing.'

Paternal, he may have been, but with some of the characteristics of a Victorian father. 'I did not often come into contact with him but he sometimes came into contact with me,' Charles Ritchie (1849–53) remembered. Various forms of corporal punishment, however, were general at schools of the time (King's College School under Major was a rare exception). In Edkins's class Fagan remembered the 'daily drawing of the figure of Euclid, Book 1, Prop. 5, on the board for the benefit of an unfortunate who could not learn it, and the daily flogging which followed till the ass had crossed the bridge'. In 1842 there was a complaint about Edkins and from then onwards masters were in theory required to obtain

The Revd Dr George Mortimer, Headmaster 1840–1865.

Ten of Dr Mortimer's 16 children were at the school. Down and across: *Bust of Dr Mortimer; Alexander Mortimer, barrister; Frederick Mortimer, banker; Col. Henry Beaufoy Mortimer, Assistant Adjutant-General of Bengal; and Col. Louis G. Mortimer.*

Mortimer's permission to cane, but Joey Harris (who took the Latin Class for 51 years and was the most affectionately remembered master of all times) was one who did not comply. Abbott remembered the way in which 'all those not personally concerned in the raid, delighted to see [Harris] set off on one of his expeditions down the long room, with a sleeping boy in his eye and a cane in his hand, to cause a rude awakening'. Harris also had in his classroom 'a certain polygonal box . . . converted into an Altar of Sacrifice' on which he would punish not only his own boys but others who, when they passed the door, would deliver 'runaway knocks'. Then members of his class would help in the ritual.

Mortimer himself also carried out public beatings. William Aldis (1851–7) remembered 'looking with great awe on the first flogging I ever saw'. But this was apparently on the buttocks with a cane, not across the back with a birch, because he continued, 'For small offences boys were caned across the hands, otherwise they knelt down and received the punishment *a posteriori*'. William Soulsby (1861–6) remembered that Mortimer 'caned me once, but in such a half-hearted way as to lead me to think that my offence was unimportant'.

In honour of his appointment Mortimer persuaded the Committee to extend the Easter break to a full week, and from then onwards the School year was divided into three terms. Other changes soon followed. That year the School was opened to the sons of parents who were not City freemen or householders. The following year the number of Carpenter scholars was doubled to eight and they ceased to board at the School. In 1843 the Lord Mayor's attendance at the School's annual Prize Day became an official date in his calendar (as a result of his cancelling the year before). At this event in 1844 he ceremonially unveiled the statue of John Carpenter, sited on the School's main staircase which led from the ground to the first floor. Fagan, who had a reputation as the School poet, read a poem (lost), and the head boy praised Carpenter in prose. Reporting the event the *Illustrated London News* noted that the School was now open to Jewish boys, something which Mortimer had made possible by exempting them from prayers and divinity lessons. 'I always had a great regard for Jewish boys,' he told the Taunton Commission in 1865, 'and I found they were not received at any schools.'

Meanwhile the School began to flourish academically and to score an increasing number of university successes, many of them at Cambridge in mathematics. According to Ulric Rule (1851–8), when Mortimer heard of some of these honours 'he was so excited that, going out of the (Sixth Form) room to tell one of the other masters, and not noticing that the door was shut, he walked bang against it with his spectacles on'.

Such achievements were in part the consequence of a range of scholarships and exhibitions which the School was soon able to offer. The earliest of these had a curious origin, described by Emery, its first winner:

> Just before I was ready to go . . . to the university *The Times* newspaper, or rather the principal proprietor of *The Times*, had done a great service to Europe and the nation. At very large expense and unsparing labour he had sought out and put to flight a number of conspirators who were trying, in a most subtle and daring way, to deceive and rob the merchants and bankers of Europe. A large subscription was raised in order to repay the proprietor of *The Times*, old Mr John Walter, his expenses, but fortunately for me and for a great many others he said, 'No, I have done it for the public good, not with the idea of any remuneration at all, or of having my expenses repaid. What you have raised you had better therefore give to a good public object.' Some excellent Common Councillors or Aldermen thought there should be a great statue or a great clock erected as a memorial, but better counsels finally prevailed, and in 1841 one scholarship was founded for the City of London School, and another for Christ's Hospital to be called *The Times* Scholarships. I was the first boy to win ours . . . I used to be invited to attend the annual prize-giving in the theatre of the City of London School, and, if I may say so, was a sort of show boy there for some years.

Above: *Joey Harris, who took the Latin Class (so named because it was not Greek) for 51 years.*
Below: *Impression of the statue of John Carpenter after its unveiling at the school in 1843.*

Other leaving scholarships and exhibitions followed, among them in the 1840s the Tegg Scholarship to Oxford, Cambridge or London University and the Salomons scholarship, established in 1845 by the first Jew to become Sheriff of the City of London. In the 1850s came a large number more, including a medical scholarship in alternate years at St Thomas's Hospital, and two founded by City companies: the Goldsmiths' Exhibition and the Grocers' Exhibition. Only Merchant Taylors' School was said to have more leaving awards. All were over-shadowed by the gifts of the School's most generous early benefactor, Henry Beaufoy, not only in value but in the influence they had on the School.

Both Beaufoy and his father, Colonel Mark Beaufoy, were distinguished engineers, Fellows of the Royal Society. Henry, the son, had received his award for experiments in the rifling of gun barrels. He had also inherited the family vinegar and British wine business at South Lambeth. In 1843 the family solicitor, Francis Hobler, presented a pair of dies to the School for striking medals for mathematics, to commemorate the 'scientific attainments' of Henry Beaufoy's father, Colonel Mark.

Why Hobler should have done this at his own expense is a mystery, but he probably hoped to ingratiate himself both with the Beaufoys and with the Common Council by patronising its school. He had friends on the Council and his own father was retiring that year after 40 years as clerk to the Lord Mayor. If this was his plan the result must have far exceeded his hopes, for his gift interested Beaufoy, the son, in the School and next year Beaufoy gave it the first of four scholarships, worth £50 a year each, for mathematics at Cambridge. Of the 21 boys who won Beaufoy scholarships during the next 20 years, 19 became wranglers.

Beaufoy was a shy, self-effacing man, and when, in gratitude, the Common Council had his portrait painted, he in return gave the School a painting in which he himself did not appear, but solicitor Hobler was shown presenting the deeds of

35

his seventeenth birthday, but the School thought that he was too young for Cambridge life, so kept him another year, reading excessively difficult mathematical books without tuition. This nearly destroyed his interest in the subject, but he survived to do pioneering work on the foundations of modern pure mathematics. He formed with his wife, Grace, a unique mathematical partnership, publishing jointly over two hundred research papers in the first quarter of the twentieth century. Cuthbertson held the two positions of head of mathematics and Second Master for 33 years before he died suddenly in church.

There is even less doubt that the School was ahead in the teaching of science. In 1845, seven years after William Cook's brief period of lectures, Mortimer reminded the School Committee that the subject had been promised in the School's regulations, and made detailed suggestions for its reintroduction. Some of the second-floor rooms which he was leaving could be used for the purpose. Eventually, however, Thomas Brewer, School Secretary, came to live on the second floor and space for science was found in the basement.

This space consisted of a storage room and, more importantly, a passage, closed at each end with glass doors, which became known as the green tunnel and which led directly to the Theatre's arena. It was here, in March 1847, that the Revd Thomas Hall, newly appointed chemistry lecturer, gave his first lecture.

Hall had been on the staff since September 1837, first as an assistant writing master, then as a form master. Why he was chosen and what he knew of the subject have been forgotten – perhaps he learned as he taught. However he managed, he turned out to be an inspired choice. The feature of his teaching which put it years ahead of that at other public schools was that, although he still delivered lectures, he also involved the boys themselves in practical scientific work. William Perkin (1870–7), writing about Hall's teaching of his identically named father, said that Hall had the green tunnel fitted up as a laboratory and used it principally as a preparation room for his lectures, but here he would also 'suggest simple experiments and encourage boys to carry them out at home, and afterwards he himself would examine the substances which they had made'.

Perkin the father (1851–3), who was only 18 when he discovered the mauve aniline dye on which the coal-tar dyeing industry was based, confirmed this. As a small boy he had already begun to 'accumulate bottles of chemicals and make experiments' and when he was sent to the City of London School he found to his delight that 'lectures on chemistry and natural philosophy were given there twice a week. 'These I attended, and not long afterwards the lecturer, seeing the great interest I took in the science, made me one of his lecture assistants, my duties being to prepare the experiments, arrange the table, and assist at the lectures. The dinner interval was the only time I had for fitting up apparatus and preparing for these lectures. The lecturer was Mr Thomas Hall, BA, one of the class masters, and he was very kind to me and helped me in every way. My father [a builder] was disappointed at my choice, and the outlook for chemistry was indeed very poor in those days; but Mr Hall had several interviews with him, and eventually I was allowed to follow my bent.'

As for modern languages, the speeches of boys at Prize Days, always made in French and German (as well as Latin, Greek and English) confirm that the School continued to treat them seriously. Delille remained an outstanding French teacher

Distribution of prizes by the Lord Mayor to the boys of the School, 1844.

until 1858, when he was succeeded by his assistant. Though German was still an optional subject, Bialloblotzky's successors caused fewer problems.

The School was ahead in another way, Fagan claimed. It 'set the pattern' in having 'separate classrooms ("the Prussian system" we used to be told)'. If this was not strictly true – King's College School had separate classrooms from its opening in 1831 – these were certainly years when most public schools, new and old, still had large halls, in different parts of which different masters would try to teach their classes. The City of London School was also unusual, Fagan considered, for the commitment of its masters. 'They didn't look on collecting blue china or rare bartolozzis as the end in life, and the making of money by school-keeping merely as a means to that end. They hadn't even time to write about schoolmastering, so busy were they with the work itself.' Certainly Old Boys had warm memories of most of their teachers and remembered few if any with bitterness.

Conditions nevertheless remained primitive. Boys came to School through the filthy streets of Dickensian London, often inches deep in mud. Above this in Cheapside in the 1840s wooden pavements were laid with consequences which were equally unpleasant. In hot July days

when we were panting for green fields and the great exam. of the year was coming on, the dust used to rise, palpable to taste and smell, higher than the first-floor windows, churned up by the perpetual whirl of carriages. No wonder a boy living there without a bit of playground, with no games but what we got up for ourselves – boxing till we were dustier than millers, or singlestick – should have worked by fits and starts, chiefly for exams. In

Opposite page: Pages from the *chemistry notebook, kept at the School, of William Perkin, discoverer of aniline dye.*

39

Old Boys could become honorary members. By 1862, however, it had suffered the first of three collapses, not to be refounded until 1865. Then, or perhaps from the start, Mortimer made it 'almost a requirement' that boys who joined should be able to swim, and this may have restricted its membership for this was not then a general accomplishment.

The club had always, however, had more general sporting purposes, hoping from the first to be able to obtain 'a playground for the permanent use of the School'. And though this did not happen for many years, the School's first cricket club was founded in the spring of 1861, receiving from the failing Rowing Club its remaining funds. By this time Vardy had gone to Cambridge, and the Cricket Club's main founder was Seeley, now back from Cambridge to teach at the School. On 11 May 1861 the *City Press* reported:

CITY OF LONDON SCHOOL (Surrey Side). This new club commenced the present season on Saturday last, with an afternoon's practice at the Surrey Cricket Ground, Kennington-Oval. Although this club has only been established a fortnight, the number of its members exceeds thirty. Among them are several youths who give promise of becoming first rate cricketers. The days for practice are every Wednesday and Saturday at three o'clock.

The term 'Surrey Side', probably implied that only boys living in Surrey could belong. The club seems, however, to have played its matches not at the Oval but, like other London schools, wherever it could rent a field – Battersea Park, Tufnell Park, Victoria Park, Hackney or the Eton and Middlesex ground near Primrose Hill. It was well enough supported to hire a professional, and in 1864 for the first time played against a team of Old Boys.

A football club followed in 1863, playing soccer at Victoria Park. Next year it changed its game to Rugby, under the influence of Vardy, back from Cambridge after a short period living with Anthony Trollope as a tutor to his sons. Vardy was later to become the Chief Master of King Edward's School, Birmingham, where a boy described him as 'a short thick-set man, generally wearing heavy boots and planting his feet very firmly . . . He seldom raised his voice; his rebukes were solemn, never hasty or exaggerated; he was always punctual, never in a hurry, always deliberate, never flurried.' During his time as a master at the City of London School he took holy orders, and can be seen as the sort of games-playing cleric that many public schools acquired in the 1860s and 1870s.

Next year the first issue of a school magazine reported, 'A match was played on Wednesday Nov. 30, with the sixteen of Dulwich College, and as it came off on their ground we conceded them most of their rules, including their novel and difficult "off side", which has now been dropped even at Rugby. After a good game we were beaten by one goal.'

Vardy was also largely responsible for starting school athletics, which were organised by the Cricket Club; he gave a guinea for prizes, to add to the three guineas given by the master he had replaced. Thus games and sports of various sorts were flourishing by the time Mortimer left and he must take credit for encouraging them. The School had 'an extensive' football club, he told the Taunton Commission, and a cricket club of 170 members.

In Mortimer's time it began to have other features which did not become general at public schools until two or three decades later, one of them an Old Boys' club. This had been started in 1848 by an ex-head boy, Henry Hose (1837–45), and four or five friends at Cambridge. Back in London the same group held one or two trial dinners then, in October 1851, officially constituted itself as the Carpenter Club.

Its general purposes were to keep Old Boys in touch with each other, and to create a benevolent fund to help dependants or orphans of Old Boys, but it also maintained close contact with the School. Mortimer, Vardy, Joey Harris and Hale were all at different times its annual president. It gave the School two history prizes, and at Vardy's suggestion, two athletics prizes for hurdling.

The School's first magazine only survived for two issues (December 1864 and February 1865) before disappearing for 12 years, leaving its funds to the Cricket Club. It was a slim affair, of pocket book size, selling for 6*d.* and including the first two episodes of an ambitious serial, 'Pierce Hamildowne; or, Preparatory School'.

Its modern curriculum remained the feature which made it remarkable, and this was recognised by the Parliamentary Commission on Endowed Schools (called the Taunton Commission to distinguish it from the Clarendon Commission which had already reported on the country's nine leading public schools). The Taunton Commission published its results in 1867, but its inspector, D. R. Fearon, a well-known figure in the educational world, visited the School and interviewed Mortimer in the June of 1865, his final year. It was thus in effect his own school report, and it could hardly have been a more flattering one. Among 'schools of the first grade', Fearon wrote, the City of London School was 'by far the best pattern of what a London school of that grade ought to be, and which more than any other school in this district will repay careful study and attention'.

Joseph Sharpe LLD, first treasurer of the Old Boys' Club, and a law professor at University College London.

Mortimer was able to tell Fearon that it had 637 boys and a waiting list of 240. (In 1839, Giles's last year, it had declined to 336.) He also reported the results of an interesting survey he had carried out among parents of 73 boys of the upper school. Thirty-seven were professionals (doctors, lawyers, teachers and clergymen), the remaining 36 tradesmen. It was this division of the School into boys from two different classes whose parents had different ambitions for them which Fearon considered the School handled with such remarkable success. It contained, he wrote,

> two distinct classes of scholars, viz., those . . . who leave at about 18 for professions, and those who leave at 16 for business . . . It is thus both a superior and a secondary school, and covers a very wide educational field. It therefore becomes interesting to notice how the school manages to combine the sort of education required for those entering the universities and liberal professions with that demanded by those who are going at 16 into business. [Such a school was] commonly considered to be placed between two fires, and to be in an awkward position. On the one hand it is pressed by the demands of the universities. If it wishes to win their laurels it must give a place to the study of the dead languages; a process which sacrifices the education of the many and indeed of all scholars of the second grade, for the

*Dr O. Froembling, German master
from 1860.*

*John Spillar, examiner in chemistry at
the School in the 1860s.*

sake of a very brilliant result with the few . . . The most common attempt to reconcile these conflicting claims is by means of the process called 'bifurcation', a difficult and hazardous process . . . The City of London school has, at any rate, not attempted it. How then does this school get over the difficulty?

I believe it will be found that the secret lies in the following circumstances:
(1) The staple of the school instruction is science . . . Arithmetic, mathematics, and chemistry form the bases of the intellectual nutriment.
(2) The study of the dead languages is deferred to a later period than is usual . . . Latin is not begun with boys until they are on the average 12fi years old, and . . . Greek is not begun until they are on the average 15 years old. The boys have been previously well grounded in arithmetic, French, and perhaps also German, and received some elementary instruction in mathematics and chemistry. Their minds have been opened, they have begun to think and compare. Latin and Greek can now be taught them on philological principles; they make rapid strides, and by 18 or 19 they have just as good a chance of being elected to open scholarships at the universities as if they had begun the dead languages at the age of eight or nine years.

Fearon next complimented the School on its 'graduated admission examinations' and asked how it managed to maintain the quality of the 'good material' which these produced. By the 'removal system', he wrote; 'that system of removing boys who, without committing any heinous school crimes, do not try to keep up with the fair average mental and moral growth of their companions'.

Fearon's two criticisms were of features beyond Mortimer's control and the result of Corporation parsimony. The classes were too large (five of the 12 classes numbered 60 or more, the top class in the junior department 80) and the pay of junior masters too low (£120 to £130). This was confirmed by Farnell who arrived the following year. 'The masters of the lower forms were not inspiring; one did not meet the type of "the schoolmaster and the gentleman" on the staff until one reached the fourth or fifth form.'

Mortimer admitted that salaries were low, but not that the masters were inferior. Asked why, he said, 'we are only able to command first class talent from the universities, owing to the attachment of Old Boys to the School . . . Old Boys will come back for £200 a year less than they can obtain elsewhere.' To this Fearon added 'the satisfaction of working in a brilliant and successful School under an able and successful headmaster'.

Fearon also commented on the fact that the School's masters were chosen not by the Headmaster but by the Governors. Mortimer replied that in practice the School Committee had never ignored his advice or appointed a master without his approval. Without precisely approving, Fearon wrote that 'on the whole the system does not seem to work badly'. He ended by repeating that the City of London School was 'by far the best among the secondary schools of London'.

It was appropriate that in 1865, the year of the visit of the Taunton Commissioner and of Mortimer's retirement after 25 successful years, Warren Stormes Hale should be Lord Mayor. As a celebration he invited the whole school on 2 February, anniversary of the School's opening as well as his birthday, to a champagne supper at the Mansion House and, according to the School magazine, all 637 of them came. As a result they had 'the honour of creating, with their cabs and carriages, a block in front of the Lord Mayor's residence, and greatly hindering traffic between King William Street and Poultry'.

In the Egyptian Hall James Wrenalds (1858–64), a bright boy but probably a poor one since he never went to the university, spoke for the School, and the Lord Mayor made 'a very gracious speech' in reply. The company then toured numerous scientific side-shows – these were the years of the Great Exhibitions of 1851 and 1861 and Hale shared the general interest in science and technology. In the saloon 'the magnesium light, under the direction of Alonzo Grant Esq., . . . glared full upon some couple who had flattered themselves on enjoying sweet converse unobserved', while in the drawing room was 'exhibited, on the screen, by Dubosq's lantern and electric light, a splendid portrait of the Lord Mayor'. At the same time in the Egyptian Hall a juggler juggled and a Mr Jester performed so splendidly with his doll that 'loud shouts of laughter continually drowned the voices of the accomplished ventriloquist and his melodious aunt'.

Meanwhile,

The Venerable Lord Mayor mingling, like our kind Headmaster, with the crowd of happy boys, seemed to delight in their delight; . . . whiskered fellows in the 6th fancying themselves men, were talking with the masters . . . ; young hopefuls in knickerbockers and the first junior were jostling against students who were in four years to be high wranglers or Chancellor's medallists.

After nine, supper was announced on the first floor, and the provident immediately proceeded thither fearing the rush that came in time. Batch after batch went up, batch after batch came down, chanting the charms of the champagne and chicken, singing the savour of the salad, bepraising the boar's head, and alluding to the Lord Mayor as a (hiccup) brick. Some were so bold as to try to get somebody else to dance. They failed as they deserved. Others executed to perfection the strains of 'We won't go home till morning'.

J. T. Ablett, appointed in 1854, stayed for 37 years, one of a series of long-serving masters at the School.

6

To the Embankment with the Great Doctor Abbott

1865~1889

Edwin Abbott Abbott, Headmaster 1865–1889.

Edwin Abbott Abbott – only 26 when appointed to succeed Mortimer, so young and slightly built that he was sometimes mistaken for a member of his own Sixth Form – had ideas of his own about improving the School, formed when he had been a boy there, but he was also strongly influenced by his close friend, John Seeley. There were good reasons for his taking advice from such an experienced friend. Seeley was not only four years older and had been head boy when Abbott arrived at the School in 1850, but from 1861 to 1863 had taught there and was now Professor of Latin at University College, London. They had another connection. That year (1865) Seeley's *Ecce Homo* had appeared, published anonymously because of the daringly fresh view it took of Christ's life, but Abbott had discovered the author. 'This bond of a common secret,' he remembered, 'brought J. and myself very much together; and we used at that time to spend one evening a week together; and not one of these evenings passed away without my gaining something to think about, some new seed of truth.'

Some of these seeds of truth Seeley described in an article three years later.

> A boy goes to school, [he wrote] and at fourteen he is taken away, having read a book and a half of Caesar's *Commentaries*, two or three epistles of Ovid, and a book of Xenophon. In his mind at the end of this time, what images have been deposited? There are some chaotic conceptions of Caesar exhorting his troops, and of Grecian soldiers marching indefinitely through Asia at the rate of so many parasangs a day. What happened when these soldiers reached their destination it is likely enough he has never found out, because that is recorded in another part of the book. Towards cultivating his imagination and taste, towards enlarging his contemplations, this is all that has been done.

Criticisms of the teaching of the classics were not unknown by this time. The previous year Frederick Farrar, author of *Eric or Little by Little*, future Master of Marlborough, had expressed them even more vigorously to members of the Royal

The masters in 1887. The second row includes (from left) V. T. Ablett, W. G. Rushbrooke, Dr F. Cuthbertson, Dr Abbott, Revd J. Harris, J. R. Dicksee and T. Todd. In the row behind, H. Dicksee is fourth from the right.

Institution. But Seeley had positive proposals. To replace Latin before the age of 14 there should be a 'common education', and a large part of this should be scientific.

> But it is not of this I would speak now [he continued]. I do not quarrel with the principles of the classicists, but with their means. I would reach their goal, but by a different way. I think they are right in the importance which they attach to words, but I would substitute English words for Latin ones. I think they are right in introducing boys to great works of genius, but I would substitute modern genius for ancient. In a word, I advocate a comprehensive and elaborate English education.

It was, of course, enormously useful to Abbott that changes of this sort had already begun under Mortimer. Not only had the teaching of Latin and Greek been virtually eliminated in the lower school but, more importantly, the Beaufoy prizes had established the study of English Literature in the upper school. Abbott later claimed that he was careful at first only to 'perambulate' his new school and to avoid giving the impression that he planned to change everything, but everything did not need changing, and in fact he acted comparatively quickly. By 1869 he was able to claim that his was the only public school in which the study of English grammar and of such writers as Shakespeare, Milton and Scott was part of the curriculum in all classes.

From the start he had re-established in full the awarding of the Beaufoy prizes. Under Mortimer these had at first been awarded in all three categories: recitations, essays and examinations in the texts, and Mortimer had even written to Beaufoy with a further suggestion. 'What do you think of adding . . . the performances of certain scenes from the Plays, which may be got up and practised at leisure in the Theatre of the School during the twelve months preceding?' But Beaufoy's influential solicitor, Hobler, disapproved, considering it a mistake to introduce 'theatricals' into the School, so 'turning the boys' heads upon such subjects instead of graver subjects', and adding when he sent back the draft of the deed, 'I flatter myself I have cast out entirely the idea of making the School a vehicle for the Drama'. Furthermore, the recitations themselves had apparently lapsed. Now in 1866 Abbott revived them and

Sir John Robert Seeley KCMG, Composition Master at the school, later Professor of Latin at University College London, afterwards Regius Professor of Modern History at Cambridge.

arranged for them to be delivered and judged annually before an audience of parents and boys on Beaufoy Day, when the essay and examination prizes were also awarded. And during the next few years the recitations developed into the performances of scenes. According to William Rushbrooke (1862–8, later a master for 11 years at the School then head of St Olave's, Southwark) Abbott himself rehearsed the boys, 'and astonishingly well he did it'. In 1868 Asquith played the Bishop of Carlisle in *Richard II* and Orleans in *Henry V*, as well as taking part in a French play.

On Beaufoy Day 1883, the first to be celebrated in the School's new building, a consecutive performance was staged: the first three acts of *Julius Caesar*. Even then, however, no costumes were worn, indeed a prologue, said to have been written for the occasion by Abbott, included the lines:

> Rome is our theme today, yet we confess
> We have not here one shred of Roman dress;
> Our properties are none, our scenes are nought,
> We have but Shakespeare's words and Shakespeare's thought.

'It may be fairly said,' the Magazine reported, 'that the success was much greater than could have been expected on the first attempt of this kind.'

Subsequently recitations became once more the usual form of the competition, but these were often judged by visiting celebrities. In the 1890s Beerbohm Tree and Henry Irving came in successive years. With or without 'theatricals', Beaufoy Day was firmly re-established from the start of Abbott's time as an important annual occasion.

Farnell summarised the effects of Abbott's transformations:

> Even in the lower forms, and long before I came into personal contact with our headmaster, Abbott, I enjoyed unconsciously the benefit of his influence. In his educational theories and outlook he was in advance of the other teachers of his time.
>
> He at once made fruitful reforms in the traditional curriculum. In the first place he was passionately devoted to English Literature and was himself a considerable Shakespearian scholar; therefore he made the study of a good English book part of the terminal work of all the forms, and hereby I was brought into contact early with many of our masterpieces, especially with Shakespeare, whom I had already learned to love; and on my own experience I can give the lie to the often-expressed view that boys are alienated from our great authors if they are made to study them as part of their school tasks. It was certainly by this method that very many of us were brought to know and to love many of our great ones, Scott, Wordsworth, Shelley, Tennyson, and more than all, our Shakespeare.

Opposite page (clockwise from top left): Henry B. H. Beaufoy FRS, one of the School's most important benefactors (portrait by H. W. Pickersgill); Illuminated manuscript from the School expressing thanks to Beaufoy for his generosity; Warren Stormes Hale, called the Second Founder of the School (by Derek Fowler); and the Rt Hon. Herbert Henry Asquith, Prime Minister 1908–16, later Lord Oxford (by R. H. Campbell).

It was not only for English Literature that Abbott and Seeley were passionate advocates but for the English language, both its grammar and how to write it. In 1871 they published together *English Lessons for English People*. In its dedication (to Mortimer) they wrote that although schools were now taking up the teaching of English and it formed an important part of 'most Government and other examinations', there was 'a complaint from many teachers that they cannot teach English for want of textbooks and manuals'. The book was intended to fill this gap. An example of its message comes in the preface where it warns against what Fowler,

35 years later, called 'elegant variation'. 'There is a temptation to shrink with a senseless fear from using a plain word twice in the same page, and often from using a plain word at all.' Next year Abbott published *How to Write Clearly*, forerunner of such books, lectures and essays as Fowler's *The King's English* (1905), Quiller-Couch's *On the Art of Writing* (1916), and George Orwell's *Politics and the English Language* (1946), arguing against the obscurities and double-speak of academics, bureaucrats and politicians.

Old Boys of Abbott's time whose subsequent careers suggest the influence which English teaching at the School had on their lives included Walter Raleigh (1874–6, Professor of English Literature at Liverpool, Glasgow and Oxford), Israel Gollancz (1877–82, the first University Lecturer in English at Cambridge, then Professor of English Language and Literature at London University), and Sidney Lee (originally Solomon Lazarus; 1870–8, a renowned Shakespearian Scholar, co-editor with Leslie Steven of the *Dictionary of National Biography*). When Lee died Gollancz wrote of him that 'his pride was ever in the School, to which he owed the inspiration which moulded his whole life. It was a noble throng of Sixth Form boys who with him caught from Dr Abbott the enthusiasm for English studies which produced such outstanding achievements in the field of English – and especially Shakespearian – scholarship.'

Opposite page: *The Second School, on the Embankment, 1882–1986 (oil painting by Norman Wilkinson).*

Others of this throng were Henry Beeching (1872–8, theologian, poet and anthologist), Arthur Bullen (1867–75, founder of the Shakespeare Head Press, refounder of the *Gentleman's Magazine*) and Charles 'Paddy' Montague (1879–85) who, with C. P. Scott, made the *Manchester Guardian* the prestigious paper it became and who wrote *Disenchantment*, one of the more important books about the First World War. To serve in that war Montague, aged 47, dyed his white hair, and reached the trenches as a sergeant, before being invalided out. 'Some men's hair,' said his fellow journalist, H. W. Nevinson, 'turned white with fear but Montague's had turned dark with courage.' About Abbott Montague wrote, 'To be taught by him is the most fortunate thing in my life . . . He could simply trans-fuse a sense of the fineness of great poetry from his own mind to a boy's . . . his *English Lessons for English People* . . . must have raised literature from the dead for thousands of schoolboys.'

Though Farnell was a classicist, he was equally grateful to Abbott for maintaining and expanding the School's science teaching.

> Another original departure that he [Abbott] made from the prevalent curriculum was the institution of a school laboratory and the inclusion of the elements of physical science in the timetable of all the classes . . . feeling the greatness of the scientific achievements of the age, he did his best to make us feel it. Therefore all through my eight years at school I attended a chemical or 'physical' lecture or demonstration for one hour every week. Of course throughout this long period I learnt no chemistry or physics; for a boy can learn nothing definitely if he only gives his mind or half his mind to it for one hour a week. But I learnt what Abbott probably wanted me to learn, a respect for these studies and for those who follow them and a vague impression of hidden worlds. Therefore when I came into contact at Oxford with the conventional classical scholars of the average public school type who called all these things 'stinks', I felt that they marked themselves down.

The school laboratory to which Farnell referred was for a class in practical chemistry which Abbott announced at the 1869 Prize Day. Two years earlier the Mortimer Scholarship in Chemistry and Electricity had been founded, the money subscribed mainly by Old Boys. The same year Thomas Hall finally retired, after 22 years as the School's first and only science master.

He was succeeded by Henry Durham, who had come to the School as a laboratory assistant, and Isaac Scarf. These two, like Hall, had had little scientific education, and yet for over 40 years taught the whole range of science subjects from chemistry and physics to botany, zoology, and geology, a period during which the telephone, flying and anaesthetics, to name just three inventions, were to transform life. Durham retired in 1910. 'He always wore a smart frock coat, tightly buttoned . . . very frequently while lecturing he used to close his eyes in an ecstasy of intellectual joy, but he was always sufficiently wide awake to detect any of our social efforts.' Durham was an addicted pipe smoker, at a time when smoking in the commonroom was forbidden, and would sit by the chimney so that this would carry away the smoke.

Scarf finally left in 1919, so equalling Joey Harris's 51-year record. When he died two years later the Magazine wrote, 'He was a fine type of an elder generation of devout and humane scientists, more appropriately called natural philosophers (in Scotland moral and natural philosophers), and a lineal descendant of the "learned and curious gentlemen" of the eighteenth century.'

Twenty years later, after the move to the Embankment building, one boy remembered that

> Science in the eighties meant to the greater part of the School Durham's lectures. Of course . . . there was also Scarf, who was credited . . . with knowing five times as much about Science as did Durham. But, he could not put it across. He lacked the rhetorical, almost theatrical style with which Durham could invest the most commonplace fact of Chemistry with an almost mystical significance. You seldom got bored with Durham. Even if you did not take in what he was saying, you watched his gestures and listened to the modulation of his voice . . . The original Lecture room . . . was capable of holding about half the School. It had some twenty tiers of benches sloping up almost to the limit of vision and easily accommodated the three or four classes of the Middle School . . . With such large numbers attending, one or two more or less made no odds. Daring spirits sometimes cut the lecture, and took their chance of being challenged in the playground. In a corner of the room there stood a large model of the School building, dissected to show the heating and ventilating arrangements; it had won a medal at the recent Health Exhibition. A small but enterprising youth once took a lecture tucked away in the great hall of the model.

Future distinguished scientists of these years included Perkin's two sons, the identically named William Henry (1870–7, who established chemistry as a respected subject at Oxford and was considered the greatest organic chemist of his time), and his brother Arthur (1872–8, Professor of Colour Chemistry and Dyeing at Leeds University); and Frederick Hopkins (1871–6, winner of the Nobel Prize for Medicine in 1929).

Abbott not only extended the teaching of modern and scientific subjects but transformed the School's classical teaching by connecting it to a general study of languages and their interconnections. Farnell remembered that Abbott was 'caught by the enthusiasm then prevalent at Cambridge for the study of philology, at that time in its interesting and easygoing youth.' He provided better teaching in it for the scholars of his Sixth Form than they could find for many years afterwards in the lecture rooms of Oxford; for this purpose he introduced his advanced classical pupils to the study of Sanskrit.

To teach Sanskrit he imported George Nicoll, later Professor of Arabic at Oxford, described by Farnell as 'more like a gnome than a man'. Abbott gave a prize for Sanskrit, of which Sidney Lee was one of the winners. When a certain Lord Mayor presented the prize for this dead language to another winner he said that he hoped it would be useful to him in India.

There were also, of course, divinity lessons, as a result of which Farnell believed that he 'brought up to the University a more exact knowledge of the more important books of the Old and New Testament than did the average classical scholar'. Neither Farnell nor other boys of the time seem to have been aware of Abbott's earlier religious problems. Just as Seeley, in *Ecce Homo*, tried to bring his belief that history should be a science to the story of Christ, so Abbott tried to reconcile his belief in science with the Resurrection and other supernatural Biblical events, only succeeding (in his own view) after much doubt.

Impressive and ahead of their time as Abbott's modernisations of the curriculum were, they do not on their own account for his reputation because they leave out the special nature of his own teaching. Boy after boy was inspired by his spirit of earnest endeavour, describing him as the best of all headmasters, and their time in his Sixth Form as the formative period of their lives.

> Apart from any of his special interests and reforming ideas [Farnell wrote], it was his whole personality that inspired and controlled us. The strong soul power within him he could impart to others: and this is the mark of the spiritual leader. He was aflame with intellectual energy, and he kindled those who were under him. He never drove us or overtasked us; but he made intellectual effort a kind of religion for us . . . My three years in the Sixth were the happiest of my school life, happiest in the intellectual sense, because I was conscious of new mental horizons opening up . . . I have a pleasant memory of that young society of the VI Form, intellectually keener and more enthusiastic than any undergraduate society that in the next few years I came to know.

For Bramwell Booth (1868, son of the founder of the Salvation Army) Abbott 'was really the first person to awake in my mind any definite idea that I might be able to do something. He kindled a little flame of aspiration.' And Asquith told a meeting of the John Carpenter Club, 'I could not easily find words which would do justice to . . . all that I owe him.'

Abbot did not *teach* his Sixth Form in the normal sense, but engaged with it in a co-operative search for the truth. He made this search

> a game in which the whole class could join all the time and every time, each member of it to the full extent of his capacity . . . one of Abbott's commonest

Opposite page: Annotated diagrams from a chemistry notebook made by a boy in 1872. Dr Abbott included physical science in the timetable of all the classes.

Henry Durham, who succeeded Thomas Hall as Science Master in 1869, and stayed until 1910.

51

methods of dealing with a muddled answer was to turn to another boy and make him repeat the explanation given; and when it appeared that the muddle had produced a still worse muddle in the second boy's mind, Abbott would look back to the first boy and say 'You see how far you have made him understand.'

None of us will ever forget those construing lessons. To say they were interesting is nothing; they were keenly exciting. He nearly always walked up and down the room and when a boy in construing approached a serious difficulty he would balance his little figure finely upon the tips of his heels, slightly swaying with controlled eagerness, and listening intently. If the boy faced the difficulty and got through, the soles of his feet would come down rapping the floor smartly. 'Good!' he exclaimed; and we all felt that one summit of the mountain had been safely crossed. (Robert Conway, 1875–83, later Professor of Latin and Indo-European Philology at Manchester University)

Abbott extended his co-operation with his class to its behaviour, thus, as Beeching put it, reconciling 'discipline with freedom'. If some fresh offence was committed he would say, 'Here is a new crime; do not let us be arbitrary, let us fix some suitable penalty.' When a penalty had been agreed he would say, 'Let it be understood, then, that this is always to be the penalty for that offence.'

Designs for stained-glass windows for the School, 1886.

In spite of Abbott's reforms, the School retained Victorian characteristics. The junior classes were still enormous, and often primitively conducted.

[T]here was a remarkable method of class management in those days . . . The master might put a question to the top boy and if he could not answer it he passed it rapidly down the ranks till some one gave the right answer: this might be boy No. 70, who then found himself transferred from the depths and placed at the dizzy height of 'top' where if he was clever and industrious he might maintain himself. It involved a vast displacement of ranks and much promiscuous shoving dear to the hearts of the young, and much interruption to the lesson. But it was almost as pleasant as a game of 'Snap-tongs', which it much resembled, and it added a sporting element to many a weary hour.

For Abbott's first 18 years the School was also still in its old Milk Street building, as crowded and ill-equipped as ever. The classrooms were 'illuminated by flaring and unshaded gas jets, and as the height of our desks bore no relation to the height of the boy sitting there, most of us were wearing spectacles before we left' (Farnell). And in spite of the various games clubs formed in Mortimer's last five years, most boys still discovered their own forms of physical exercise. Outside the School building Walter Raleigh remembered, 'best of all "tig", carried on among the traffic in Cheapside. I can't believe that any playing fields can provide a sport to equal this' (presumably an early form of 'Chicken'). Inside the school he had 'epic memories of wars between the Latin and the Third when the separating door was opened (probably without permission) in the intervals between hours. In these wars two boys fought with an abandon and fury I have never seen surpassed, at the business of taking and rescuing prisoners.' And in the Horseshoe, 'one class would have to defend the steps while another would try to storm the steps' (Charles Young, 1869–74).

There continued, however, to be games and athletics for boys who wanted them, supported by clubs which somehow overcame the difficulty of the School having no ground, but which would periodically have to be refounded. Of these the Cricket Club was least successful, disappearing for seven years between 1869 and 1876. The Football Club, now playing an early form of Rugby (only goals or converted tries counted), was more successful. In Young's time 'it would play against University College School and Godolphin School among others. We used to play at Victoria Park, and changed in a tavern . . . I have a recollection that we indulged in shandy gaff after the game.' John Steggall (1868–74) remembered boys walking to Primrose Hill or Victoria Park 'from many different homes' then returning on foot 'perhaps sleepy, certainly tired, yet happily discussing the event of the week, and fit to do our work for the next day'. And his contemporary, Robert (Billy) Allpress (1870–4) remembered that great match of the year (strongly resembling the game described by Hughes in *Tom Brown's Schooldays*) in which the Sixth Form played the School.

The sides were unlimited, but it was rarely that the Sixth exceeded fifteen, while the School was often sixty strong. By sheer weight the Sixth forwards would be pressed back towards their own goal, till an heroic back went down on hands and knees, with his head well tucked in, right in the track of the surging mass; over went the whole lot, and great was the fall; but somehow no one was ever killed or even seriously hurt.

In 1874 the result of this match must be very nearly, if not quite, a record. The Sixth were fourteen, one man short; the School were about sixty. The Sixth won by seven goals and seventeen tries to nothing.

In 1874 the Rowing Club had been refounded.

Our headquarters were at Kew [Farnell remembered], and twice a week we rowed in fours from Kew to Teddington; for in those days the tide swung up to Teddington without a lock. I got to realize the delight of trying to row well, the pain of struggling up against the tide and the joy of the swift return in the full ebb of it. I came also to find that no solitary athletic accomplishment is so fascinating as watermanship in a racing skiff; the very word recalls to me long and lonely reaches of the upper Thames and the silken surface of water flushed with sunset over which one's skiff skims on an even keel – if one had got the mastery – between banks of whispering reeds. Thus my life-long love of the Thames began in my apprentice days in the School Boat Club.

And from 1865 at the latest there had been an annual sports day, usually on 24 May, Queen Victoria's birthday. In 1867 this was held at Beaufort House, Walham Green (Vardy the starter), but more often the Lillie Bridge ground at West Brompton was used. For five shillings a boy could enter for every event. In 1872 Young (just 16) remembered that

[T]here were two bigger and much older boys, Maybury and Lee. The latter had thick whiskers and beard and looked quite forty, and they were both trained athletes. I had never thrown a hammer before, but I got the prize. Maybury and Lee, who had thrown further than I, had gained so many prizes that, only being able to take three each, they were barred from taking any other. By a little judicious diplomacy I got them to give up that prize.

Asquith, at the School from 1864–70, was already an orator at that time.

By 1860 the School had a Sixth Form Discussion Society. When Abbott attended he would take the chair – and correct exercises while he listened – but not while one boy was speaking. Asquith was already an orator in a different class from his school fellows: Abbott remembered him as one of the few boys who 'could plunge into an intricate and involved sentence with such an artistic prescience of what he had to say, that all the members of the period fell, as it were, into harmonious co-operation, so that in the end he brought his hearers to a full and satisfactory conclusion without any sacrifice of point, force, and, above all, of clearness.'

Asquith taught himself public speaking by attending trials at the Old Bailey. 'Again and again he was to be seen there, eagerly following the speeches and watching the procedure of counsel in cross-examination.' His oratory did not make him universally popular. 'I'm afraid some of us . . . were disposed to criticise him, as he was rather inclined to talk above our heads and use long words' (Joshua Vardy, 1864–9, younger brother of Albert). William Angus (1864–9, later Professor of Latin at the University of Wales) was more appreciative.

The style of his speeches differed from that of the ordinary schoolboy's as that of Macaulay's history differs from 'Little Arthur's'. We were not too young to feel the contrast and forecast a brilliant future for the young orator.

Even then it was not fire or passion . . . but the fine phrasing, the elaborate periods, the ambitious rhetoric that impressed us . . .

I remember when I had assigned to me the task of making a Prize Day speech in French in honour of the pious Founder, whose praises were sung in five languages, I exhausted my own small powers in devising something new on so well-worn a theme and then button-holed Asquith for copy. Without hesitation he gave me out of his own superfluity (having the Greek speech himself to provide) a succession of brilliant paragraphs.

From 1877 there are records of the motions discussed by the Sixth Form Debating Society, as it had now been renamed. ('National compulsory Education is Unjustifiable' – defeated 8 to 6. 'Museums should be opened on Sundays' – carried 12 to 7.) This was the year in which the Magazine, after a 12-year gap, reappeared, its 12 issues suggesting much stored-up literary ambition. By 1889 it was appearing at the more modest rate of two issues a term. During that first year School Notes mostly reported university scholarship successes or the fortunes (commonly misfortunes) of the School's sports clubs. The remaining pages consisted either of fiction, at first home produced, later joined by serialised episodes of a Jules Verne story, or of articles of general interest. The first editorial was immediately followed by a well-informed description of the misfortunes of 'Servia'. Issue No. 7 reviewed one of Fitzgerald's early translations of Omar Khayyam. In December 1884 it reviewed Abbott's celebrated *Flatland*, a description of a two-dimensional world as seen by one of its polygonal inhabitants, written perhaps to suggest that our limited view of reality left space for a religious view. Though Abbott had called himself 'A Square', the reviewer clearly knew the author's identity. The pen name showed typical Abbott wit. His last two names: Abbott Abbott = AA = A^2 = A Square.

Flatland was dedicated to 'The Inhabitants of SPACE IN GENERAL . . . In the Hope that . . . the Citizens of that Celestial Region May aspire yet higher and higher to the Secrets of FOUR FIVE OR EVEN SIX Dimensions Thereby contributing to the Enlargement of THE IMAGINATION And the possible Development of that most rare and excellent Gift of MODESTY Among the Superior Races of SOLID HUMANITY.' The 100-page book appeared in November 1884 and a second slightly revised edition appeared a month later. It then went out of print in England, but was revived 40 years later because of widespread interest in time as a fourth dimension in Einstein's theory of relativity. Abbott's student William Garnett wrote in his introduction to the 1926 republication of *Flatland*, 'When a great truth comes to light, it is generally found that there have already been prophets crying in the wilderness and preparing the way for the reception of the Revelation . . .' During the last 100 years mathematicians and physicists have increasingly recognised that Abbott's little book is still the best introduction to the geometry of higher dimensions.

Within a year of Abbot's arrival the event which was to be the most important of his time – a move to a new building – was first discussed. Numbers at the School had grown steadily under Mortimer, as had the expectations of parents, and the crowded, ill-ventilated and insanitary Milk Street building now seemed less and less acceptable. So did the School's position, at the centre of the City of London,

Laying of the Foundation Stone on the Thames Embankment, 14 October 1880.

poeticised by mist, the towers of Westminster are always attractive, and towards evening there are Turnerian sunsets.' 'From the School's windows,' the Magazine wrote, 'we could trace the long broad sweep of the Embankment down to Charing Cross, the royal road for all swift vehicles, from fleeting hansoms to reckless railway vans.'

The site consisted largely of land only reclaimed from the river since the Thames Embankment Act of 1862. The Embankment thus bounded it to the south, while a new road, John Carpenter Street, formed its western boundary. Immediately to its east stood de Keyser's tall Royal Hotel, on the site now occupied by Unilever House, while it reached inland as far as Tudor Street. On the inner part of this site Wren, after the Fire of London, had built a theatre, which was used by various companies for the following 40 years but eventually pulled down soon after 1720. Since 1814 it had been occupied by the Imperial Gas Works. Remains of theatre and gas works were found during the School's construction – and again a hundred years later when the inland parts were demolished.

The School itself was built in Renaissance style. Steps led up to an impressive front door flanked by stone columns, into the entrance hall with Abbott's sunlit study and the library on the left and the School Secretary's study and the Committee room on the right. Ahead the Grand Staircase rose past Carpenter's statue, then divided, both branches turning back to reach the building's finest feature, the Great Hall. This magnificent room stretched across the full width of the building's first floor, 100 feet in length, 45 feet in depth, 60 feet high with an open timbered roof. Including its gallery it could accommodate about 1,000, though only 816 in the body of the hall, which was fitted with 'permanent seats of a peculiar construction . . . balanced and hinged to fall back, as at some of the theatres, and every alternative row has a further movement by which the back of the seat becomes a desk for the occupants of the seats immediately behind'. These lasted until the 1970s when they were replaced by 540 less peculiar but more comfortable seats.

The classrooms were contained in a long wing which ran back from the main building and faced John Carpenter Street. The *City Press* complimented the School Committee for 'very properly' making them 'an example of the most advanced theory in modern class room planning'. Each had a lock-up desk, these so designed that 'no boy, however bent on mischief, will be able to shake his neighbour's desk'.

'Mindful,' the article continued, 'that the education of the playground is one of the peculiar advantages of English public schools, which tends to mature the manliness of character distinctive of British boys,' the School Committee had provided a covered playground which occupied almost the whole of the School's basement, this 'cheered by walls of white glazed brick', and for an outdoor playground the whole area not occupied by the L-shaped School buildings. At one side of this six fives courts and a gymnasium provided remedies for long felt needs.

The new City of London School on the Embankment, as it appeared at its opening in 1882.

than performing them. On 6 March 1885, however, it staged the first recorded complete play at the School: Euripides' *Medea*. Charles Montague played Creon. 'The costumes,' the Magazine reported, 'though improvised and therefore somewhat rough, produced on the whole a good effect . . . *The Children* were dressed in the requisite minimum of clothing. They were very natural in life, and, after some effort, managed to rise to the occasion of simulating death.'

By June 1880 the Fourth Form's Natural History Society had created a museum which included 'a good collection of geological specimens'. Five years later it reported receiving gifts of coins, shells, butterflies, a razor-bill's egg and a specimen of sugar cane. In October 1880 a Sixth Form Literary Society was established, describing itself as a lineal descendant of the Debating Society but with more comprehensive aims, these to include 'the reading of papers on various subjects'. For some years there had also been a Fourth and Fifth Forms Debating Society and in 1885 this developed into a 'parliament', boys taking the parts of such leading politicians as Gladstone, identified only by the names of their constituencies. It was a time of political excitement, and much interest was taken in such events as the First Irish Home Rule Bill of 1885 and the death of Gordon at Khartoum in 1886.

In the debating societies and the parliament William Rushbrooke took a leading part, indeed for some boys he was as memorable a master as Abbott. Anton Bertram (1881–7) remembered that when he summed up debates 'his speech had the effect of a steam roller, crushing and flattening out all that had been said on the opposite side. He did not . . . produce the impression of rigid impartiality which emanated from Dr Abbott.' To Charles Myers (1885–90, Consulting Psychologist to the British Armies in France during the First World War) it seemed that

> No master ever realised more fully than he now much could be done in educating his boys outside the class. He used to encourage us to visit and report on notable ancient buildings in London. As a sort of Speaker, he ran once a week after school hours a model Parliament, in which we boys played the part of cabinet ministers or of the opposition, carefully preparing and rhetorically introducing bills on topical matters.

Though Rushbrooke supported games, he was no fanatic, and an influence for treating them sensibly. 'We see in some places,' he told the Representative Assembly, 'an excessive worship of athletics. I am glad to say that in our School, at least, athletics have not been carried to excess. They have always been subordinated to School work, and that is as it should be.'

Though the School prospered in its new buildings, there developed during Abbott's last two years a fierce debate about its curriculum. This began in 1887 when a member of Common Council, T. H. Bartlett, tabled (to use Abbott's words) 'a revolutionary proposal . . . in favour of making certain changes in the School curriculum, which should be carried out at the cost if necessary even of the extinction of the classical languages. I am amazed at the proposal,' Abbott continued, 'considering that it was the desire of our founder that his "four poor boys" should proceed to the universities' – a remarkable claim from someone so devoted to the truth, since Carpenter's bequest (as given by Don) did not include the word 'poor' and said nothing about a university future for his boys.

Opposite page: *Stained-glass windows, showing the arms of benefactors, originally in the Milk Street School, then in the entrance hall of the Embankment School, and now in the dining hall of the new School.*

William G. Rushbrooke took a leading part in the debating societies at the School, collaborated with Dr Abbott in his work on the Synoptic Gospels, and went on to become Headmaster at St Olave's, Southwark.

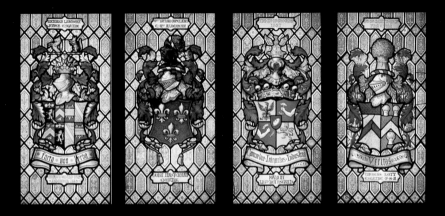

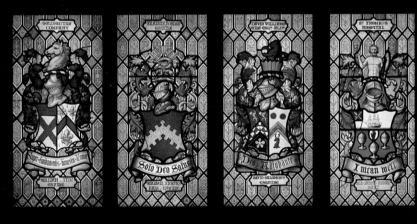

Abbott was not against further modernising the already comparatively modern curriculum, and now proposed his own changes (which included making German a regular subject, though at Prize Day 1888 he added that no one should be worried that such changes would 'lead to the extinction of the higher classical or mathematical studies').

Throughout the argument Abbott gave public thanks to the chairman of the School Committee, Frank Tayler (1847–51). It was Tayler who had 'successfully opposed' Bartlett's original motion and carried an amendment. In October 1888, by which time Abbott's changes to the curriculum had been introduced, it was Tayler who had defended 'the best interests of the School . . . in recent debates before the Common Council'. And in July 1889 Abbott told the John Carpenter Club that it was 'largely owing to the able representations of their President [Tayler]' that the recent crisis' had he hoped 'successfully passed, and an altered scheme of work been adopted which 'avoided the evil of sudden, premature, and dislocating changes'. 'The very prospect of a second agitation,' Abbott continued, 'of which he had heard some incredible rumours, had brought parents to him' asking whether the School's character was to be changed.

The rumours were not incredible, as Abbott must have known, because the Common Council's vote of 20 September the previous year asking the School Committee to establish classical and modern sides at the School had been discussed again in October and November 1888, in spite of the introduction of Abbott's changes. Furthermore, four months before he now spoke, on 13 March 1889, he had already resigned.

No doubt Abbott felt that after 25 years he had given the School the best he had to give it. He may also have been wanting time to compose the many religious works which he spent the next 35 years writing. But his letter of resignation makes clear that the real reason for his resignation was the Common Council's demand for a commercial side at the School. The heavy burden of office, he wrote, 'has been increased by the important changes in the course of study introduced by the court last year, changes which – though beneficial in themselves, if well controlled and directed – require increased rather than failing powers in the Headmaster.' There is also little doubt that he disliked any scheme which would allow even half the upper school to abandon the classics.

He was persuaded to stay until the end of the year, and during this time continued to take part in the controversy, pointing out in November in a letter to the School Committee that it had already caused damage. For the first time during his regime the School was not full. The reason, he thought, was that many prospective parents believed that it planned entirely to sweep away its higher department and give simply a 'commercial education'. They were 'delaying to send their sons, till they are reassured on this point'. Even if parents did not wish their sons to go to the university but to enter some profession, they wanted them 'to associate with others who may hereafter be connected with the universities'.

He added, 'It would have been indeed more pleasant for me personally to have terminated my labours last Michaelmas . . . Then I should have been spared the pain of reporting a diminution of numbers, concerning which I will venture to say, without fear of contradiction, that it has been caused not by any action on the part of the present Headmaster, but rather in spite of his utmost efforts.'

Opposite page: The new School from across the river.

65

For as long as any of Abbott's pupils lived they wrote and spoke of him with a gratitude and admiration almost certainly warmer and more unanimous than that felt by Old Boys of any other public school for their headmasters, either before or since. When he died in 1926 Steggall wrote,

[M]any old pupils have recognised and still recognise with a feeling approaching awe, the unparalleled influence of Dr Abbott upon the lives and characters of them all . . . For me, as for many others, a brilliant and helpful light has been, for a short time we believe, darkened; leaving us for the brief remainder of our lives without the presence of him to whom slackness, sloth and deceit were almost unpardonable sins.

Right: *Dr Abbott in a contemplative pose;*
Below right: *His resignation letter from the School, 13 March 1889.*

7

The New Century:
Commerce and Journalism

1890~1905

ARTHUR POLLARD, Abbott's 36-year-old successor, the School's first lay headmaster, came from Yorkshire and had taught at Oxford High School and Dulwich College before, only the previous year, being appointed Vice-Master of Manchester Grammar School. His north country accent was a gift to School mimics, and his obstinacy and impulsiveness were to trouble his employers, but his 15-year regime included many important developments, in particular the restructuring of the School which he had been appointed to undertake. In May 1890, when he had been in office only one complete term he reported to the School Committee on the changes which would 'give effect to your desire to provide at the City of London School "a thoroughly Commercial Education for those who may desire it, without in any way prejudicing those who may wish to be educated on the lines followed before the recent alterations were made".'

Only the middle and senior schools were affected, all boys in the junior division continuing to have one curriculum. At the top of the School the Classics Side retained its old Sixth, Fifth and Fourth Forms, with below them the senior and middle removes. There was now, however, an alternative Modern Side, with the old Latin class as its senior form and above this the Modern Fifth and Modern Sixth Forms (though these were described as 'in prospect'). Below on the Modern Side came forms now called Old III, II and I, and New III, II and I.

On the Classics Side French and natural science remained among the regular subjects, with other modern languages optional. On the Modern Side Latin remained an optional subject. Allpress, summing up the new arrangements in the *Public School Magazine* of November 1898, wrote, 'It will be seen that boys on the Classical Side can learn any subject that is taught on the Modern Side, while boys on the Modern Side can learn any subject taught on the Classical Side except Greek. A more elastic scheme could hardly be devised.'

These changes were not easily made, Pollard's chief difficulty being a lack of competent modern language teachers. Abbott had already had to recommend that Monsieur Caumont be given an official warning because of 'the disorder' in his

Arthur Pollard, Headmaster 1890–1905.

R. H. 'Billy' Allpress, the effective head of Modern Side.

class. Pollard's policy at first was to revert to English teachers of French and German, a feature still usual in many English schools, though originally one which the City of London School had avoided. The fact that Harris, who now became the senior Modern Side master could only teach mathematics and English subjects was a further difficulty, and in practice he became a figurehead, with the Modern Side headed by Allpress. 'I had Mod IV when I was appointed in May 1891,' Allpress wrote, 'and took over Mod V in September 1892. Mod VI was not created till some time later and was just an adjunct of Mod V for boys who deserved promotion.'

Though these senior classes on the Modern Side developed gradually, they indicate Pollard's foresight. 'Modern' was the word he used, in contrast to the word 'Commercial' almost always used by the Corporation and the School Committee. And though his inclusion of bookkeeping and shorthand in its regular subjects showed that to some extent he was prepared to provide what they wanted, from the start he was anxious that this new part of the school should not be seen by parents as inferior, nor its boys despised by the School's classicists. In November 1890 he asked the School Committee to stimulate the Modern Side by 'establishing a Scholarship or two, say of £50 or £60, to send boys abroad for a short period to the country which they choose, after they have received their preliminary training in languages here'. Perhaps he already foresaw a time when Modern Side boys would win modern language scholarships to the universities, as one, William Wetenhall (1900–6) eventually did, to Caius College, Cambridge.

The earliest beginnings of a Science Side were remembered by Myers, a classicist, who eventually decided

Conversaziones were staged from 1890 to show parents and outsiders the recent improvements at the School.

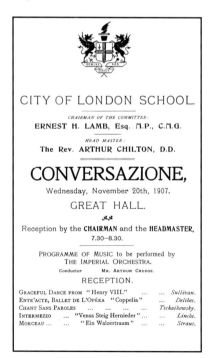

to ask permission to prepare under Durham's tuition for an Entrance Scholarship examination at Cambridge in Natural Science. Henceforth I was excused much of my ordinary class work. I worked with Durham in physiology as well as in chemistry and physics. As boys in such circumstances always do, I discovered quickly enough that Durham knew little more physiology than I did, and that he was always reading my textbook a few chapters ahead of me. But he was a kind, if not extremely competent teacher, and took endless trouble with me. I was, of course, the sole member of his class; indeed I may thus in a sense . . . claim to be the first boy on the Science Side which was established on my departure.

It was then (1891) that Pollard announced grants from the Common Council of £1,500 to promote science teaching at the School and build a physics laboratory. Owen Glynne Jones was appointed as a physics teacher and in January 1892 the Science Side duly opened with 20 boys.

The remodelling of the School suggested to the School Committee the holding of 'an entertainment to enable parents and outsiders to obtain some notion of the structural improvements of the last two years'. The first such entertainment, called a conversazione, was staged on 17 December 1890 – 'fortunately before the influenza had come upon us' (Magazine). Exhibits and displays in different classrooms included a phonograph which 'very successfully reproduced' a solo on the cornet, a humorous recitation and a march of the Coldstream Guards.

The conversazione became an annual event, attended in 1899 for example by 2,200 guests. That year it included as usual a gymnastic display, a concert 'of a very high order provided by friends of the Chairman' and for the first time a Cinderella Dance in the Great Hall, 'for those guests who cared for it and they were in a majority' (School Committee report); to accommodate this all 816 seats 'of a peculiar construction' had to be unscrewed and removed.

If this annual event had something of the nature of a modern parents' evening, the School had already (1886) modernised itself more radically by abolishing Saturday classes. Many London day schools (Highgate School and King's College School for example) took almost another hundred years to do the same, and then only after anguished debate.

In 1897, to commemorate the fiftieth anniversary of the start of science teaching at the School by Thomas Hall, a 'Hall Memorial Fund' was launched. The largest contribution (double any other) came from the Worshipful Company of Leathermakers, of which Dr William Perkins, the discoverer of aniline dyes, was the Master. Other contributors were Perkins himself, his son of the same name and the astronomer William Huggins. The Magazine took the opportunity to mention five more Old Citizen Fellows of the Royal Society, one a professor in Dublin, another in Calcutta, another in Japan.

First mention of the Boer War by the Magazine appeared in December 1899, in the form of a letter from Alfred Symonds (1871–5), describing his escape from Johannesburg to British controlled territory in a sheep truck. By the following April it was able to name 26 Old Citizens 'now at the front'. Meanwhile, in January 1900 George Steevens (1882–8) had died of enteric fever during the siege of Ladysmith. Of all nineteenth-century boys at the School (with the possible exception of Asquith) Steevens was the one of whom greatest things were expected. His six-page obituary in the Magazine told how, 'when he was a boy of fourteen in the fifth form, one of his schoolfellows drew up a list of the careers suitable for each boy in the class to adopt when he should leave school. Opposite all the names but one there was written something more or less humorously disparaging. Opposite the name of Steevens there was the word "genius"; and when the paper was handed round, no one felt that the description was misplaced.'

The Boer War in general and Steevens's death in particular had significant consequences for the School. In 1900 a School Corps was formed. Public school corps had first been formed in 1860, in response to a call from Palmerston for a volunteer army of 150,000 to guard the country against a threatened French invasion, but a proposal to create one at the City of London School had been rejected by the School Committee. In May 1880, however, before the move to the Embankment the Magazine reported that 'A (City of London School) Company of the London Rifle Brigade Cadet Corps would hold parades at the School at 3 o'clock on Tuesday and Friday afternoons.' 'Prospectuses and full particulars,' it continued, 'may be obtained from the Cadet Sergeant during drill hours at the School, and orders for the week are posted on the notice board outside the Porter's Room. Private Fisher (of the Latin Class) and Bingemann (late of the School) have been promoted jun. and sen. Lance Corporals respectively.'

The company does not seem to have flourished, and had disappeared by the time Pollard, at Prize Day 1900, announced a School Corps. Later that year (3 December) this drilled for the first time; and on 15 May 1901 Col. Matthew of

G. W. Steevens, war correspondent, who was trapped in the siege of Ladysmith, where he died of enteric fever in 1900.

the London Rifle Brigade inspected it, 116 strong, in the playground. Speaking afterwards he said that 'he was pleased to see the boys knew how to stand still – that was the first thing a soldier had to learn. He was specially pleased with the way in which the corps was booted; all the boots were most excellent, and just the thing for military work.' He was persuaded, he added, 'that the training of boys in school was the answer to the question of conscription'. These were years when the question of conscription, in order to match the vast conscript armies of Germany and France, was much discussed.

The Corps went to summer camp for the first time in 1901, and provided a 62-strong guard of honour for the Lord Mayor in 1903. The same year a shooting eight was formed, which entered for the Ashburton Shield, coming last of the 42 competing teams. The truth is that in these early years, although the School Corps had enthusiastic members it was not the important feature of school life that it had become at many public schools, and by 1905 its numbers had shrunk to 49.

The consequences of Steevens's death were more remarkable. At first he had worked on the *Pall Mall Gazette*, but in 1896 had been recruited by Alfred Harmsworth, the future Lord Northcliffe, as an ideal correspondent for his newly founded, empire-celebrating *Daily Mail*. Since then Steevens's articles on Germany, the Greco-Turkish War and above all Kitchener's reconquest of the Sudan, which were the basis of his best seller, *With Kitchener to Khartoum*, had made him the country's best-known young foreign correspondent and an obvious choice to send to the South African War. Northcliffe was so distressed by his death that he hurried to Clapham and 'prostrated himself in front of Mrs Steevens, crying in a loud voice that he had killed George by "sending him to Ladysmith".'

As a further atonement he made a substantial gift to Steevens's old school to be used to promote the study of journalism. When this was announced at Prize Day 1902 it was said to come from 'an enthusiastic journalist'. The Chairman of the Schools Committee added that it was natural for 'the gentleman concerned' to turn to the School because of its curriculum and because of the number of pupils it had whose fathers were journalists. The gift was partly to be used to fund an annual scholarship worth £400 for the boy who had shown greatest journalistic promise, 'to go round the world, so as to gain . . . an actual acquaintance with the details of journalism . . . especially in the United States and in the British dominions beyond the sea'. It would be known as the Steevens Scholarship.

In the journalism classes, conducted twice a week after school by William Hill, editor of the *Westminster Gazette*, boys learned reporting, editing, leader-writing, make-up and reviewing. The class also produced its own magazine, the *Steevens Gazette*, which included historical events described as in a police report. Hill's son, also William (1899–1905) was the second winner of the scholarship, and Leopold Spero (1899–1907, later to write *The Dreamer*, a novel closely based on the School) was the third.

The class produced a number of successful journalists, including Walter Hirschbein (1899–1906), who changed his name to Hurstbourne during the First World War when he worked for Northcliffe on *The Times* – evidence of the School's connection with Northcliffe's well-known wartime propaganda. But according to Spero the number of entrants for the scholarship declined from ten in 1902 to six in 1903 and three when he won it in 1904. The following year Northcliffe withdrew his support for the whole scheme.

70

The School suffered two losses in these years – one inevitable, the other shocking. In 1892 Joey Harris finally retired. He was already part retired, teaching only about eight hours a week, and it was as a master of the Latin class in Milk Street days that he was remembered. This had been almost as much a club as a class; in the lunch break Harris would organise boxing and single-stick – when he wasn't taking a service for boys at a nearby church. One member, Henry Jones (1878–81), remembered that Harris 'always sat under an open window . . . and wore his pot hat to keep the draught from his head'. Jones gave an example of the sort of Joey Harris joke which seemed at the time so hilarious. 'I have often wondered,' he told Old Boys, 'how I am going to occupy my time after I retire. This morning I was walking up Aldersgate Street when I noticed in a shop window the following announcement, "Muff Stuffers Required" and it struck me that I had found what I was looking for, as that was exactly what I had been doing all my life.'

Harris's 51 years had not only included the complete regimes of Mortimer and Abbott, but also the teaching of Abbott in the Latin class, and when he died in 1892 it was Abbott who wrote his obituary for the Magazine.

> What also struck me [Abbott wrote], was the suddenness with which Mr Harris would sometimes rein himself in on any occasion when he felt that he might be in danger of hurting anyone's feelings . . . It was this broad and general sympathy . . . that attracted us to him . . . He was essentially a 'club-bable' man in the best sense of the term, always trying to make the best of any two or three fellow creatures in whose company he happened to be.

Seven years later (1899) the School lost Owen Glynne Jones, after only eight years as its first physics master. Besides being an able teacher, Jones was an outstanding mountaineer, who would circle the common room without touching the floor (apart from the impossible crossing of the fireplace). He and the Second Master, F. W. Hill, became mountaineering companions and were climbing the Alpine Dent Blanche when one of their guides slipped, the rope broke and all three guides

'The Last of the Latins': part of a framed picture presented to Joey Harris on his retirement in 1892, showing the boys from his last class, drawn by one of them, W. S. Hegdemann.

Owen Glynn Jones, physics master, was also a climber in the Alps, Snowdon and North Wales. He died in a climbing accident in 1899.

together with Jones fell to their death. Hill survived, though only after spending 50 hours on the mountain, with just a few raisins for food, sleeping with his ice axe pressed against his stomach to save himself from falling.

It is no absurd exaggeration to suggest that, if Hill had not survived to inspire a brilliant mathematical pupil, Max Newman (1908–15), Germany might have won the Second World War. Newman's first achievement was to inspire a Cambridge student, Alan Turing, to write a paper in which he described the first computer, never in fact made but now known as a Turing machine. When the war came Newman, Turing and two other Old Citizen mathematicians, Derek Taunt (1931–6) and Bernard Schultz (1925–34, later as Bernard Scott founding professor of Mathematics at the University of Sussex) all worked at Bletchley Park. There 'the most successful intelligence agency in world history' was responsible in particular for breaking the German Enigma Code, an achievement of which the importance can hardly be exaggerated. The work of Newman's team, which led directly to the development of electronic computers, has only recently become known. For security reasons records were destroyed and it remained secret for 30 years.

Throughout Pollard's time the School's search for a playing field continued. Grounds at Balham, Wandsworth, Denmark Hill and Willesden were tried but found unsatisfactory before, in October 1894, a fairly good football field at Beckenham Hill was discovered and rented, though it was not suitable for 'serious cricket'. Graham Smith (1890–9, future Headmaster of Sedbergh), had a 'vivid picture of fielding in the MCC match in the position which today would be called "in the gully". A hard cut hit the ground a yard in front of me, and stopped dead in a hole.' Nevertheless on a fine half holiday some 80 to 100 boys would go there – a reasonable number considering the distance some boys had to travel to school and the half hour journey they had to make, on a branch line of the London, Chatham and Dover railway to reach Beckenham Hill station. The Beckenham ground was also used by Old Boys, who, Allpress wrote, 'are exceedingly "clannish", and hold together in after life. There are no fewer than three associations.' The original Carpenter Club of 1851, renamed the John Carpenter Club, had been supplemented in 1880 by the Old Boys' Reunion, its object to enable younger Old Boys to keep in touch with each other and to encourage them to join the John Carpenter Club. More recently (1894) the Old Citizens' Athletics Union had been formed, to support football, cricket, fives and athletics among Old Citizens.

For a time the Beckenham ground seemed adequate, but it had no pavilion and space for only three simultaneous games, and in mid-November 1901 these disadvantages caused the Schools Committee (as it was now called after the founding of the City of London School for Girls in 1894) to lose no time in 'acquiring for the School a permanent site for Athletic purposes. The Old Citizens' Athletic Union . . . would willingly contribute to its maintenance', and it could also be used by the new school's girls.

The Common Council acted with reasonable speed, deciding in principle the following year to buy a freehold playing field, the cost to be shared with Abbott's Field Fund. By May 1903 the Schools Committee was able to report that 'the work of preparing the ground is now in full swing . . . the pavilion, also, is in course of erection'. The new ground was at Catford. Not only would it have a pavilion but it was

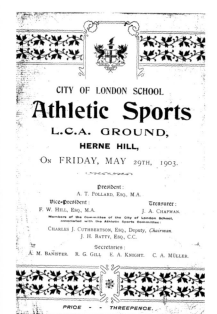

CITY OF LONDON SCHOOL.

Athletic Sports

L.C.A. GROUND,
HERNE HILL.

ON FRIDAY, MAY 29TH, 1903.

President:
A. T. POLLARD, ESQ., M.A.

Vice-President: Treasurer:
F. W. HILL, ESQ., M.A.   J. A. CHAPMAN.

Members of the Committee of the City of London School, associated with the Athletic Sports Committee:

CHARLES J. CUTHBERTSON, ESQ., Deputy, Chairman.
J. H. BATTY, ESQ., C.C.

Secretaries:
A. M. BANISTER. R. G. GILL. E. A. KNIGHT. C. A. MÜLLER.

PRICE - - THREEPENCE.

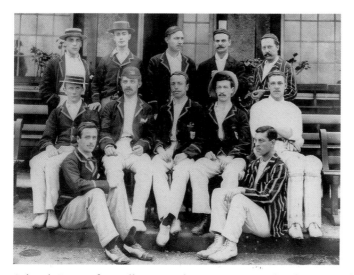

Old Citizens' Cricket Club, 1893.

closer to the School. It was formally opened on 9 June 1904, when a cricket team of Old Citizens, as Old Boys were now called, defeated a team of boys and masters.

Pollard was a lonely and not entirely happy man, Jack Marsh remembered being told by his father (they were both masters at the School). He would invite members of the staff in the evenings to play billiards with him. To the boys he was a heroic figure.

> A great human soul, a reverent scholar [Spero wrote about Paulton, the name he gave him in *The Dreamer*], who served no humbugs or vulgarians for his own profit, who set out in forthright Yorkshire what he thought, and why he thought it, who loved the School to which he had given the best of his life, and left it when they wished him to be other than he was.

A. E. Douglas-Smith (1911–7), in his 1937 history, *The City of London School*, wrote about the reasons for Pollard leaving with similar delicacy. He did, however, mention a fall in numbers which certainly declined from around 700 in the four years 1894–7 to an average of about 60 fewer for the following seven years, bottoming at 617 in 1904. And he suggested that 'rumours of the internal disagreements were affecting public confidence'. The disagreements concerned two matters: Pollard's wish to retire some of the School's elderly masters; and his resentment of the influence of the School Secretary, A. J. Austin. After 1896, wrote Douglas-Smith (the year of Austin's appointment) 'a certain friction in matters of internal administration began . . . It is said that boys were required to stand when the Secretary entered the room . . . a salute given to no one else but the headmaster.' The Schools Committee seems to have supported Austin. As part of its 1898 proposals for improved salaries it listed at much length the Secretary's duties and asked for his salary to be increased to £350, rising to £600, though its proposed salaries for the most senior masters were only £300 rising to £450.

In March 1905 a Special (Schools and Library Enquiry) Committee reported on both these questions in ways which supported Pollard. It recommended that the Town Clerk, not the School Secretary, should take the minutes of Schools Committee meetings, an important limitation of the School Secretary's powers.

Picture by Arthur Rackham (CLS 1879–83) of W. S. Pate (CLS 1887–95), who in 1895, the date of this drawing, brought the mile record below five minutes.

About the School's staff it wrote,

> it is not necessary for us to here deal with the question of the Headmastership . . . although the subject received earnest and lengthy consideration at our hands. We are glad that a satisfactory arrangement with Mr Pollard has been arrived at, and think it probable that some changes in the Teaching Staff of the City of London School for boys may be advantageously made.

The 'satisfactory arrangement', however, seems to have referred not to changes in the staff but to Pollard himself because he had by this time resigned. The previous 16 February the Schools Committee had begun the process of selecting a successor. Furthermore, on 6 July the Schools Committee in its annual report wrote about staff changes: 'The Special Committee do not indicate what changes they had in mind; but having carefully discussed the matter in all its bearings, and having recently visited every class during working hours, your committee do not see any reason for any immediate change in this direction.' And about the School Secretary's minute-taking it wrote, 'Your committee . . . are strongly of opinion that, in the interests of the School, no change should be made.'

Pollard's relationship with his employers cannot have been helped by an interview he gave to the *Saturday Review*, published in May 1903. In this the interviewer, clearly quoting Pollard, wrote about the teaching of modern languages, 'probably at the City of London School there are greater difficulties in this respect than elsewhere, for the headmaster has not free choice of his staff, the choice resting with the Committee of the Corporation which manages the School, and we doubt if the arrangement is educationally a satisfactory one'. More surprisingly, Pollard had told the interviewer that he disapproved in principle of the division of the School into two Sides which he had been required to establish and would have preferred to see 'one curriculum so as to secure the maximum of homogeneity and social unity' in the School.

By the time Pollard left at the end of the 1905 summer term the boys knew something of his problems and made their feelings clear. They presented him with a silver centre piece for his dining room table – preferable, he said in thanking them, to a travelling bag, in case someone else 'seeing so nice a bag, would like to travel with it in my stead'. And after his last Prize Day (he told Old Boys at a dinner that October) he had been

> much touched to find that the whole Sixth Form waited some long time . . . in order to give him a parting cheer; whilst on the last Wednesday of term, at twelve o'clock, when the boys usually rushed home as fast as their feet could carry them, he found to his surprise that his study and the whole of the entrance hall were blocked with boys. It appeared that in the School Magazine he had incautiously allowed a portrait of himself to appear, and these boys would not leave until he had signed each of their copies.

8

" Faber fabrum adjuvet "

War Takes its Toll

1905~1929

The Revd Arthur Chilton, 41 years old, another classicist, headmaster of Emmanuel School for the previous nine years, was to be head of the City of London School for the next 24, these to include that most traumatic of all periods for British public schools, the First World War. If, according to Spero, he irritated his first Sixth Form by imposing various petty restrictions (for example, forbidding them to hang their bowler hats on the stand by the front-hall staircase), boys and staff came on the whole to like him. But he never attracted the passionate loyalty which his two great nineteenth-century predecessors, Mortimer and Abbott had attracted, nor the similar loyalty felt for his successor, Francis Dale.

During his first term (autumn 1905) Chilton reported to the Schools Committee his general satisfaction with the School's masters, picking out in particular Hill, the mountaineering Second Master, and with the School's divided structure, now almost 15 years old. He did not mention the fact that, out of a Sixth Form of 29, there were only five scientists and one Modern Side boy. The matters he did consider unsatisfactory were, first, the excessive number of London County Council scholars, who now numbered 150. It was they who had brought the School's numbers back to 700. 'I do not forget the financial side of this fact,' he wrote, 'but . . . we must be content with fewer in future. The School is at the present moment too full, some classes containing 40 boys, whereas no class should contain more than 30.' And second, the 'somewhat chaotic' timetable. This he hoped to reform 'as soon as I have sufficient grasp of the situation to tackle such a very complicated task'.

By the following November he had tackled it and the new timetable was, he believed, working well. Its most significant feature was the reduced length of classes from 1fi hours to 1 hour, with the result that a School week now consisted of 23 periods instead of 18. Besides the subjects taught in these 23 periods boys could learn many others after the School day ended at 3.15 p.m.; indeed, in the opinion of the April 1909 issue of *The Captain* there was nothing 'from Carpentry (appropriate subject!) to Spanish, from Shorthand to Elocution and Life-Saving' that

The Revd Dr Arthur Chilton, Headmaster 1905–1929.

Boys in the Great Hall, about 1906.

The innovative Saturday Club, founded in 1904, made expeditions both locally and abroad.

could not be learned 'without extra charge'. Only for drawing, taught on Saturday mornings, was there a fee.

In 1907 the School was restructured in another way, by the division of boys into six so-called houses. The object, in Chilton's words, was 'to foster that spirit of emulation and patriotism which the division of Boarding Schools into houses had been found to produce'. The new ground at Catford provided space for the inter-house matches which epitomised such patriotism. But the change was not universally favoured by the staff, and A. J. Spilsbury, the master who proposed it, took the precaution of obtaining enthusiastic reports of the results from day schools which had done the same thing. It was Spilsbury who suggested four of the house names: Abbott, Hale, Carpenter and Seeley, to which Mortimer and Beaufoy were added.

King's College School and Highgate School, which created day boy houses in 1907 and about 1908 respectively, attempted further to encourage house loyalty by allotting boys to houses according to the districts in which they lived. Though boys of the City of London School were divided arbitrarily, this did not prevent enthusiastic masters from creating the desired house loyalty. Spilsbury himself, housemaster of Hale, was one of these, another A. G. Munro, housemaster of Seeley. First appointed by Abbott, now master of the Modern New First Class, Munro had once played as well as encouraged games at the School and had been described when it still played Rugby as a 'heavy and hardworking forward; always in the centre of the scrum'. Soccer, cricket and tennis were other games he played or encouraged, and in 1901 he helped found the School's first Swimming Club. He was not only a games enthusiast, but revitalised debating at the School by starting in 1906 the Modern Side Debating Society, and in 1904 founding one of the School's most enterprising societies: the Saturday Club. This made Saturday educational expeditions, those chosen for 1905–6 typically including Tate's sugar refineries, the East London Water Works and Greenwich Hospital, while in 1908 Munro took the Club on a ten-day visit to Paris.

He was, besides, a man of great piety. 'How well those who knew him remember his characteristic action at afternoon prayers, taken by masters in the form room,' wrote Frederick Button (1905–8), '– how he slowly and carefully took a handkerchief from his breast pocket, spread it on the dusty floor and knelt. This used to cause a snigger or two among new boys, but their attitude never lasted long.' In Spero's *The Dreamer* Munro is 'Dewar, old Badger Dewar, the grey-haired master of the Modern First, beloved of boys and men.' When he died in 1909 the Saturday Club lapsed, but an A. G. Munro Club was founded.

The house system, according to Spilsbury, had 'ramifications which I had scarcely guessed, e.g. it prompted F. W. Payne to resign the management of Athletic Sports'. Payne was one of the older masters, with no degree but much self-taught learning in English, French, German, Italian and Hebrew. He had published original research on botany, and it was in his classroom that the School's museum flourished. Spilsbury, however, did not consider athletics to be Payne's forte and approved the reforms of his successor, T. H. Knight, which brought athletics 'into line with other Public Schools'.

Though the principal house matches were played at Catford, junior matches, according to *The Captain*, took place in the playground.

> In the winter term goals are chalked out opposite each other east and west of the playground, and as there is room for at least a dozen of these, one 'team' frequently encroaches on the 'ground' of another. The games are played with small india-rubber balls, which are usually indistinguishable from each other, and many an eager footballer goes madly careering after the wrong ball, only to find his mistake when an angry class that knows him not is pouring recriminations on his head! Frequently there are two or more claimants for the same ball, and the result is chaos.

There were two other developments at the School in 1907. About the first the Magazine wrote, 'In reorganising from a new standpoint the old institution of Prefects, the Headmaster has supplied a need that for a long time made itself felt in every department of our school life' – a development which was 'almost entirely new to the School'. Though their main function was to control School games, an underlying motive must have been to give the School a feature which most other public schools had acquired, in imitation of Arnold's reforms in the 1830s at Rugby. The surprising thing is that the City of London School had made so little use of prefects before.

By this time many public schools also had a 'mission', the first established by Winchester in 1876. With the arrival of Chilton the City of London School started its own, and throughout his time it remained one of his main interests. 'We associated him very much with the School Mission,' one boy remembered. 'I have sometimes thought that, considering how much we heard about it, it was strange how vague most of us small boys were as to what it actually was . . . We regarded it as a mysterious Holy Thing with an inscrutable and quite insatiable appetite for our pocket money.' Even to those who attended the meeting of 7 February 1907 (they included Chilton, the Second Master, the senior masters of the Modern and Science Sides and the Bishops of Kensington and Dorking) the mission was still only a good intention. The association which this meeting set up had 'the object of assisting with funds and personal help some poor district in London, to be chosen hereafter'.

The chosen district was the part of Mitcham, Surrey, which became the parish of St Barnabas; it included Gorringe Park, Tooting Bec Golf Links and Ballards

The School Mission included the building of a Mission Hall and later a church.

CITY OF LONDON SCHOOL MISSION

(ST. BARNABAS, MITCHAM)

FIRST ANNUAL REPORT 1908

Boys in the School playground, about 1913.

estate, and was described as 'beautiful and open country', soon to be built over with houses for 'artisans glad to escape to this still semi-rural spot'. Here masters and boys of the School (and at first fewer Old Citizens) went to conduct a Sunday School and found a Rough Lads Club. Mr Bune, the Magazine reported, 'after scouring the streets for a night or so, managed to get quite a number of them interested. The poor fellows had a crude idea of what they were coming to, but at the same time seemed delighted that someone was interested in them. On the first night the club rooms were overflowing . . . each fellow who had been spoken to in the street brought one or two others with them . . . The lads are quite of the roughest class, but there is good in them . . . They excel in the fine art of boxing: this, together with bagatelle and draughts etc., occupied their time before the summer weather set in . . . A class is held for them every Sunday afternoon,' but the lads were 'woefully ignorant of things in general. They quite thought that Dr Chilton was coming to examine them medically, as one confidentially remarked that "he wasn't going to strip for no doctor".'

When, after six months, the mission lost the use of the Tooting Bec Golf House the need for a mission hall became urgent. In March 1908 Chilton gave a lantern lecture in the Great Hall as one fund-raising occasion. Within a year the foundation stone of the Mission Hall had been laid by Princess Louise Augusta of Schleswig-Holstein, Chilton being one of those who welcomed her, members of the School Corps forming a guard.

A church followed. In November 1913 the Magazine reported 'the walls of the new Church are rising with a rapidity which is at once exciting and alarming. All the money at present available for building is spent', a misfortune which afflicted a better-known construction project in the 1990s. By coincidence the Magazine's next article began 'The City of London School Debating Society recently passed a resolution condemning the creation of a Channel Tunnel. The Board of Trade, in consequence, commenced activities in that direction.' The Church of St Barnabas, like the Channel Tunnel, found the money it needed; by July 1914 only a further £700 was missing, in November the Building Fund was 'nearer solvency than we had dared to hope', and on the 14th of that month the Bishop of Southwark duly performed the consecration ceremony.

When Carey Oakley (1907–11, later the School's senior classics master) looked back on these pre-war years he remembered above all the way in which the Abbott tradition survived. Hard work was part of this; he had been told before he arrived 'They make you work there.' So was the teaching of English. 'Every year the Sixth were examined in Abbott's *English Lessons for English People*.' And so, despite the Modern and Science Sides, was the pre-eminence of the classics – in part as a result of the School giving it an unfair advantage. Another Old Citizen remembered that the parents of any 'top boys' who expressed a preference for the Modern Side for their sons were 'written to again and asked to change their minds'.

A bias towards the classics was typical at public schools of the time, but in other ways the City of London School was far from typical. The same Old Citizen (called 'D' by Douglas-Smith, and probably Douglas-Smith himself – only *he* passed through the exact sequence of classes which 'D' says he passed through, and furthermore Douglas-Smith was known to friends as Diggle) remembered that

After I left the School and met boys from English boarding schools I began to realise how different in many ways my education had been from theirs . . . What I value as I look back on CLS is the extreme naturalness and spontaneity of our attitude to life – to books, ideas, politics, art, human beings, and life itself. 'Swotting' was just as much of a nuisance to us . . . But it never occurred to us to consider intellectual interests peculiar. I remember arguing about Darwinism and the authenticity of the Bible all the way home with a friend, in the intervals of discussing our chances, and our House's in the Sports . . . A memory which stands out is that of a charming and very popular Sixth Former who would have been quite impossible in the average boarding school. He pursued the weirdest private studies while actually in form itself; Hebrew and shorthand among them, though he was not a Jew and apparently had no idea of any practical application of his studies. When Garrod asked him to construe he would put aside his Hebrew in almost open exasperation and translate – very ably, for he was Second Classic (as the runner-up to the Captain was in our day sometimes called) – and then go back happily to his hobby. Yet no one could have been less of a prig.

The civilised character of the School was to a large extent a result of its civilised staff. 'D' remembered that 'Very few were unpopular, and none violently so; quite a dozen were regarded with an affection which might have made any man proud.' About H. G. Garrod he wrote, 'The advent of "Gerry" in 1915 might be described as the coming of the Modern Spirit to CLS. He was of course a genuine scholar . . . but his unconventional and uproarious demeanour and phraseology must have amazed, if not scandalized, the older members of the Staff. It naturally delighted the boys.' About Spilsbury (proposer of the house system) he wrote, 'To know Spilsbury was to feel that one had made a social and intellectual advance in life . . . For all his military enthusiasm he had a widely liberal mind. I do not think any boy can ever have gone through his form without acquiring in greater or less degree an appreciation, and in the case of most of us a life-long love, of English Literature.'

Drawing beds at the OTC camp, 1914. By this date the Corps stood at over 150 members.

The Corps training at the School. From 1914, the Corps grew at once to 350 members, being made compulsory for new boys over the age of 14 in 1916.

Spilsbury's military enthusiasm had included the writing of a seven-verse song in Henry Newbolt style which the Corps adopted. Its second verse ran:

> When he's placed in his House – be it Seeley or Hale –
> Then at times he'll succeed, but at times he will fail,
> And in spite of defeats he must 'Keep up his tail'
> Till he's fit for to rank as a sportsman –
> Rank, rank, rank as a sportsman (repeat)
> Playing the game.

and its final chorus

> Trained, trained trained as a soldier (repeat)
> In your old School OTC.

Spilsbury campaigned steadily to revive the Corps after its early decline and by 1914 it had grown from less than 50 to over 150 members. Boys who would not join, 'D' remembered, were accused of slackness.

> This was true of many, but by no means all. There were many boys who played games but saw no reason for amateur soldiering and there were a number who very honestly disliked military training as a threat to world peace . . . What I liked best in the Corps was route marching through Epping Forest or Richmond Park in fours, singing. The School was very proud of its singing on the march, which was certainly far superior to that of any other school we met on field days or in Camp. The melody of 'John Brown's Body' still recalls the first time I ever heard it, with the column winding down the hill at Richmond and the lights beginning to twinkle on the River.

Left: *The OTC camp in 1914.* Below: *A similar camp at Henley in 1917 showing a City of London School tent.*

In July 1914 a contingent went to the annual camp, that year at Rugeley in Staffordshire. 'When we arrived,' the Magazine reported, 'a possible conflict between Russia and Austria-Hungary was spoken of, but we had no idea that England would be involved in it, until rumours spread that the camp cooks . . . had received orders to be ready to rejoin their regiments at a moment's notice.' Half the tents went next so that the boys were forced to sleep 16 in a bell tent, and eventually camp ended early. Within two days war had been declared. That November, in its first wartime issue, the Magazine reported the first four Old Citizen casualties.

For the next four years it listed them in increasing numbers. Many issues were prefaced with portraits, five or six to a page, of the dead. In December 1916, after the first Battle of the Somme, most disastrous of all battles for the British, there were no fewer than six of these pages, the thirty obituaries following. 'It was astonishing,' 'D' wrote, 'with what deliberate care Death went to work. It seemed that the leaders, all the best in their special ways were taken . . . the School Captains of 1912 and 1915, the Football Captains of 1911 and 1916, every Sports Champion between 1909 and 1916 . . . We got used to it. We could not always remember who were dead and who were not.'

Another who died was Laurence B. Johnson (1908–14), one of the Corps' platoon sergeants. 'English boys do not talk about death, and we never discussed the names which were read out day by day from the Platform in Hall, of those who a year before had been sitting beside us in form or playing with us at Catford. But when we heard L.B.J.'s name read out the old No. 1 platoon winced visibly, and there were a few hurried mutterings before we went into form.'

The November 1914 Magazine also listed those serving: a page and a half of officers, two and three-quarter pages of privates and non-commissioned officers – proportions very different from those of most boarding public schools, the result

81

One of a long succession of pictures in the Magazine showing those who died in the War. The portrait on the top left is of J. M. A. Hannan, who is commemorated at the School by the 1917 Society.

partly of the School's modern curriculum designed for boys who would leave school for work, partly of the London County Council scholars. Despite Chilton's early objection to so many, the number of these had increased, so that 'D', when he arrived in 1911, found that almost all his fellow new boys were from elementary schools.

> I believe this was the first batch of this magnitude. A few years later the admission of all elementary scholars was discontinued . . . My own view is that both the wholesale admittances and the entire exclusion were illogical. The scholars of 1911 so far outnumbered their other contemporaries that the chance of their acquiring whatever refinements the School had to give was endangered. On the other hand many of them were fine scholars and public-spirited athletes, perhaps the very best people in the School.

Occasionally the Magazine published letters or extracts from the diaries of those serving in France. On 4 May 1915 Alec Whittle (1906–13) wrote,

> We reached a wood some way back but still within range of guns, absolutely whacked. Our cooks had some lovely tea and skilly in the field kitchen ready for us. As we piled arms on reaching the wood I nearly burst into tears – to see the faces of our cooks and men attached to H.Q. who knew us, anxiously scanning the faces to see who was there, and the times we had to tell them of, perhaps, their pals' deaths. No. 4 Coy looked like a platoon. The Battalion casualties were well over half. At dusk we shifted to another wood and slept in the open; I was damp and we had no blankets, but four of us, together with overcoats and mac. capes, kept warm. We were too tired to be cold.

A large number of Old Citizens won awards for bravery, best known and perhaps the bravest Theodore Hardy (1879–82), chaplain to the Lincolnshire Regiment, who was awarded the VC, DSO and MC for a succession of heroic rescues of wounded men under enemy fire. Hardy had been over 50 when, in 1916, he joined the forces. In July 1918 George V, on a visit to France, presented Hardy with his VC and heard of his record. Two months later the King appointed him one of his chaplains in order to save him from more danger, 'believing his influence at home would be a great power for good', but Hardy declined the offer and three weeks before the armistice was signed was mortally wounded.

In December 1916 the Magazine published the 'now famous' letter from Eric Townsend (1907–14), already published by the *Daily Mail*, sent to his parents with instructions only to open it if he was killed.

> Dearest Mother and Father,
>   You are reading this letter because I have gone under. Of course I know you will be terribly cut up, so that it will be a long time before you get over it, but get over it you must.

Townsend went on to say that the death of a single human being was insignificant. Only one in ten million would be even briefly remembered. 'To the rest it is only granted to live in their united achievements . . . But we shall live for ever in the results of our efforts . . . I did not make much of my life before the war, but I think I have done so now.'

He ended,

Well, I have talked a lot of rot which must have given you great pain to read and which will not bring you much comfort. I had intended to try and say words of comfort, but that scarcely being possible, it has drifted into a sort of confession of faith.

To me has been given the easier task; to you is given the more difficult – that of living in sorrow. Be of good courage that at the end you may give a good account. Adieu, best of parents, – Your loving son, Eric.

Readers of the *Daily Mail* sent Townsend's parents 11,000 letters of sympathy. Today members of the School's history society place two wreaths each year at the Menin Gate in Ypres, to commemorate the School's war dead, one of them always naming Townsend.

The School itself was most noticeably changed by a great increase in the size and importance of the Corps. Its numbers rose at once by 200 to some 350, and in 1916 it was made compulsory for new boys over 14. There were also dramatic incidents. 'D' remembered that when he and a friend left the School on his last day and had walked down the Embankment as far as Charing Cross

Maroons suddenly signalled a German air raid over London . . . as it was impossible to get home during the raid, we promptly returned to the School. It was closed, but we entered through the stoke hole. Joy! Here were eight other CLS refugees assembled, and also Garrod and Mittell. We could not see them in the pitch dark, but we felt our way towards them, gathered out- side Room 1. All things were black, so the obvious thing to do was to sing. The deep hum of the German aeroplanes was soon drowned by the choruses which we sent roaring down the deserted corridors of the School . . . 'John Peel', the 'Mermaid', and the 'Tavern in the Town' rolled out, mingled hap- hazard with war-time songs . . . and Devonshire folk-songs which Garrod had introduced to the School . . . It was in the very middle of a line of 'Clementine' that the loudest and most terrifying crash of all occurred, fol- lowed by a tremendous din of falling glass . . . For a fraction of a second the voices wavered: then the old chant thundered into the darkness . . .
'But alas! I was no swimmer,
So I lost my Clementine.'
Next day we found that the Gym. had been struck, not by a bomb, but by one of our own anti-aircraft shells.

More commonly air raids occurred when boys were at home, and it was there, too, that they experienced food shortage. This made it easier for Chilton to insist that there should be little disruption of the School's normal life. Beaufoy Day, for example, was celebrated as usual, the recitations now taking the form of costumed performances.

We used to dress in the Secretary's (or was it the Committee Room?) and ascend to Great Hall by the spiral staircase from the Assistant Secretary's room. We had to be quiet in doing this, as the stair contains a first class echo, and any noise would roll magnified into the Hall above, filled with its crowd of Beaufoy Day visitors. I shall never forget our difficulty in getting

83

L. B. Johnson, as Henry the Fifth, up the stairs in his armour, our hearts in our mouths at the slightest clank.

Chilton maintained his policy to the end, refusing to let boys out of the School on Armistice Day, 11 November 1918, though agreeing that Henry Walford Davies, organist and master of the Temple choristers, who was already visiting the School weekly, should come to the Great Hall at the end of afternoon school and conduct community singing. 'The CLS Hall,' Walford Davies remembered, 'has never rung with song as it did then. It was jolly. And at the end I said to the Head, "We must cheer." "What shall we cheer for?" Garrod (after a puzzled silence) suggested the Armed Forces of the King. This was too grand and not adequate.' The boys' choice in the end was the French commander-in-chief, Foch.

Chilton remained Headmaster for another ten years, years during which his early enthusiasm perhaps declined and as a result so did the School's opinion of itself. Nevertheless, it continued to develop in important ways, one of them a direct result of the war: the acquisition of a more satisfactory playing field. The 'first agitation for a new School Ground as a War Memorial', 'D' remembered, 'came from the original members of the 1917 Society . . . We said the dead Old Boys would have wanted a new School Ground as well as Scholarships. We went and persecuted the Headmaster, the School Secretary, Sir Robert Chalmers, Mr Upjohn and others; and nothing seemed to come of it at the time. But perhaps Grove Park sprang from this seed.'

Certainly the seed germinated slowly. Though a committee of Old Citizens was formed in 1919 and decided that the funds raised for a memorial should be applied primarily to the buying of a playing field, it was another four years before the master, J. L. Troubridge, found Grove Park. 'I remember,' Chilton wrote, 'seeing a beautiful little cardboard model made by J.L.T.'s deft fingers, showing the arrangement of the grounds and running track and pavilion.' Troubridge died in 1924, before on 25 January 1925, the School's soccer XI played its first match there. On 10 July the whole school attended the official opening of Grove Park and its pavilion.

J. L. Troubridge, who planned the Grove Park ground.

The 1920s saw a wave of patriotism in the School. Corps, about 1920.

It was larger than Catford, even after some of its land had been resold, and with its pavilion (designed by Ralph Knott (1889–94, architect of London's County Hall) provided sporting facilities which the School had never had before. True, it was again far away, taking half an hour's train ride and quarter of an hour's walking to reach; and during the 1930s Jack Marsh remembered that 'We spent much time trying to whip up enthusiasm for games.' Nevertheless, School teams now often competed successfully with other public schools, at cricket and soccer, and Rugby was reintroduced. Experimental XVs had been formed in 1918–19 and had played occasional matches for the following six years, before, in 1926, the Literary and Athletic Union voted for it to become again the School game. Though it was introduced gradually, starting with new boys, by 1928–9 the School had four Rugby XVs.

These were also the early years of two new societies. One was formed in memory of an Irish boy, Max Hannan (1913–17), after he had been killed beside his disabled tank in 1918, but known as the 1917 Society because that was the last year in which Hannan and his friends had been together at the School. At first the 1917 Society had almost a spiritualist quality, Hannan's friends trying to make contact with their dead schoolfellow. But it had wider aims and greater importance in the history of the School. Its demand for a better playing field was only one of several, the others being compulsory games, services in the Temple Church, a prefects' room and a school uniform 'of a sombre hue'. Though it was some years before any of these were introduced the fact that Chilton referred them to the Schools Committee shows that they were taken seriously. 'D' traced to Hannan 'the beginnings of a wave of school patriotism which carried over into the postwar years . . . Our generation of School Prefects indulged in a sort of Purity Crusade, on which I look back with mixed feelings.' A feature of this crusade soon introduced was caning by prefects.

The School Society was also founded in 1918, its two principal founders Laurence Sach (1914–19, later a much-admired master for 14 years at the School) and Alec Coulson (1912–19, later chairman of the Schools Committee

School play by the School Society, 1920.

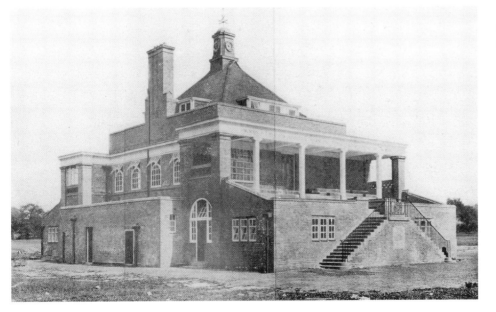

The Memorial Pavilion at Grove Park, showing the grandstand and the north side.

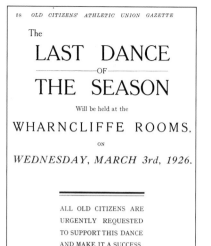

88   OLD CITIZENS' ATHLETIC UNION GAZETTE

The

LAST DANCE
—OF—
THE SEASON

Will be held at the

WHARNCLIFFE ROOMS,

ON

WEDNESDAY, MARCH 3rd, 1926.

ALL OLD CITIZENS ARE
URGENTLY REQUESTED
TO SUPPORT THIS DANCE
AND MAKE IT A SUCCESS.

'Last dance of the season': one of the activities organized by the Old Citizens' Athletic Union.

and for 51 years secretary of the John Carpenter Club), its object to promote the School's artistic and intellectual activities in the way that the (so-called) Literary and Athletic Union had since 1883 been promoting its sporting activities. The School Society organised lectures, play readings, mock trials, hobbies exhibitions, a wireless society and in December 1919, for the first time in the twentieth century, a School play: *She Stoops to Conquer.* 'One of the most memorable successes the School has seen for some years,' the Magazine reported – making 'a clear profit of £20 16s. 11d.' For a time it also had its own magazine, *The Citizen*, in reaction against the conformist School Magazine with its many pages of games reports. But, like the Literary and Athletic Union, it had no strict boundary to its activities, one of these being the organising of inter-form football matches in the playground.

Soon it played a part in sponsoring School music, one of the most welcome developments of the war years and 1920s. There had been surprisingly little music teaching or making until then, in spite of the incorporation into the School of the Temple choirboys in 1900, then of Lincoln's Inn Chapel choir (to be joined by the boys of the St James's Chapel Royal choir in 1926). Since 1881 the Magazine had reported various false starts. In March that year 'strenuous efforts' were being made 'to get up a band'. 'The singing classes,' it continued, 'which have for a year or two been conducted by Mr Hulton, have been a great success – at least, if we may judge by the pleasurable entertainments that have been given from time to time in the theatre.' It hoped that instrumental music might be taken up and that 'the present movement may not prove abortive'. On the last day of term 1889 there was a musical entertainment in the Lecture Hall, proving 'the existence of considerable musical talent, which only needs opportunity to develop', but it confessed that 'we are not as yet a musical School. There is a singing master, and class practice is a regular feature . . . of the lower part of the School, but the School, as a whole, has no musical chances. We have an organ, but it is used chiefly to provide a harmonious background for general conversation.'

The next recorded musical events were the concerts by friends of the Chairman at the conversaziones of the 1890s. Outsiders (and the occasional master) were also the performers at two concerts which boys organised in 1897 and 1898, the first in aid of the Mansion House Indian Famine Fund, the works performed being mostly songs or instrumental solos. When houses were formed a Seeley House Concert was staged for a few years, and before the 1914–18 War there were also annual Sixth Form concerts, at which it was a tradition for the School porter, 'John' (also a famous City Toastmaster) to sing 'The Fine Old English Gentleman', and 'Father M'Loy'. But it was only when Chilton asked Walford Davies to take a general interest in the School's music that more boys became involved. On his first visit 'D' remembered that 'some of the folding desks in Hall fell down, as can easily happen, making a noise. Dr Walford Davies said "I don't want those desks to bang. Now will you all bang them at once, and get it over?" The result may be imagined, and I think rather horrified the Head; but it endeared Walford Davies to us immediately.'

In March 1918 the Magazine reported that

At last Music has secured its position in the School, and the enterprise of Dr Walford Davies and his fellow enthusiasts is rewarded. A Music Committee has been formed with two members from each house . . . Each House is forming a representative quartette to take part in a House competition . . . the piece chosen is 'Early One Morning'. It has also been decided that the School shall have a song book . . . Dr Walford Davies has composed a spirited tune for the 'Carmen Domesticum' which appeared in the last number of the Mag., and this has been adopted as the School song.

The programme of the 'First School Concert' followed, and though this had included well known items like 'Green Grow the Rushes O' for communal singing, there had also been songs by the Temple choir boys, and instrumental duets and a trio by other boys of the School.

In April 1919 the School Musical Society elected its first officers. In October the first School song book was published, with 'Carmen Domesticum' (which tells the School history in verse) as its first number. Later editions gave the Headmaster and Walford Davies as joint editors. By December the Magazine could report, 'It may now be safely assumed that music has at last found its true and worthy position in the School life.'

The following July the School Society was arranging lunchtime concerts, regularly attended by some 200 boys. But it was the recording by the Temple choirboy, Ernest Lough (1924–8), in 1927 of 'Hear My Prayer', which made music at the School known to the general public. This was the first record to sell a million copies. At one time it was so well known that tourists came in crowds to the Temple Church, many of whom believed that Lough had died (and presumably been carried direct to Heaven) as soon as he had completed his recording and were disappointed to find him still alive.

The most important of all the developments of the 1920s, however, was the final emergence of the Modern and Science Sides as full equals of the Classics Side. This dated from the arrival in January 1921 of P. S. Wilkinson to succeed Allpress as the Modern Side's senior master. He was an 'immense upright figure', Donald McLachan (1919–26, first editor of the *Sunday Telegraph*) remembered, 'with . . .

The Sixth Form with Dr Chilton, 1927.

uncompromising nose, searching eyes and precise emphatic voice'. The secret of his success was that he

> would tolerate no relationship between himself and his form but . . . co-operation in the search for excellence . . . We were not asked to admire great statesmen, successful soldiers and businessmen; we were told rather of the courage and ardour of great thinkers and critics, Milton, Voltaire, Goethe, Matthew Arnold, Bernard Shaw. We were fired in one period with scorn for the philistines, for the conformists . . . the compromisers; and in the next we would be shaping our taste with the delicate graces of La Fontaine, the lyrics of Heine and Victor Hugo and the psychological subtleties of Racine.

After Wilkinson had told McLachan that he might win a scholarship he spent half an hour with him listing the novels, poetry, history, essays, biography and drama he should read. 'It was a staggering list, but I completed it – seven years after leaving the University.' Yet one more club, the 1927 Group, was formed by members of that year's Modern Fifth, while McLachlan himself represented the Modern Side's new standing by becoming the first Modern Side Captain of the School.

He was not the first non-classicist head boy, for the position had been held by the scientist Alan Clackson, in 1923–4. Now the Science Side was given a Sixth Form, as well as Science A, B and C forms leading to it. And in 1927, as a result of an extension of the School north along John Carpenter Street, it acquired new chemical laboratories, a science masters' commonroom, a new physics laboratory and soon afterwards a botanical laboratory.

If Chilton's later years were to seem a period of decline for the School when contrasted with those which followed, he presided to the end over such important changes and he was never less than a conscientious Headmaster.

The School in about 1920.

9

F. R. Dale
1929~1950

'IF EVER A KIND OF MAN vanished for good, his did' – so wrote Kingsley Amis (1934–41), not known for his tolerance of pedagogues, about Francis Dale, who succeeded Chilton in 1929. 'To hear him read Greek verse, observing tonic accent, metrical ictus and the run of the meaning all at once, was to be given a distant view of some ideal beauty . . . When the BBC . . . wanted someone to read Homer aloud on the Third Programme, they chose him.' Amis developed an imitation of the Headmaster: 'Get it right, not wrong. Black not white. Cat, not dog.' 'This . . . had the double advantage of securing esteem from classmates and providing a counterpoise to the terrified veneration I felt for my original.'

Dale, aged 46, had been classics Sixth Form master at Leeds Grammar School until 1916 then from 1920 head of Plymouth College. But the boys were more impressed by what he had done between, when, as an officer in the Royal Welsh Fusiliers (the regiment of Graves, Sassoon and David Jones), he had won both the DSO and the MC. They found him alarming. Donald Lynch (1922–30, future head of the Church Army) remembered going with the head boy, Thomas Williamson (1920–30) to Dale's study to welcome the new Headmaster. After they had spoken Dale sat staring out of the window for two minutes in total silence before answering. But they soon found that he had other qualities; he not only watched their football matches ('It was a new and rewarding experience to see the headmaster on the touchline at Grove Park'), but played cricket with them ('We had vaguely felt that headmasters could not . . . endanger their dignity by taking the risk of scoring a "duck" or dropping catches').

For some time before his appointment, [Williamson continued], we Prefects had been conscious that all was not well with the School as far as its discipline and general tone were concerned. There had been one or two manifestations of bad manners on important occasions . . . Whether Mr Dale sensed this or not I cannot say, but in his first address to the School he made it clear beyond doubt that he intended to uphold to the full the

Francis R. Dale, Headmaster 1929–1950.

authority of the Prefects in dealing with all questions of law and order. And in speaking of the Prefects, he seemed to take it for granted that it was on them rather than the Masters that he would rely.

Here was a headmaster in the nineteenth-century Arnold and Cotton tradition.

Masters reacted similarly. C. N. 'Biff' Vokins, who had taught for three years under Chilton, remembered that 'the difference was incredible'. Others considered that it was 'like going back to Abbott'.

In the School Dale's method was to wander round the form rooms, listening to the classes at work. Often he would say nothing, but occasionally he would tell some master afterwards, 'Smith in the back row didn't understand a word you were saying.' In general he might tell some master to do better, but behind this they would sense disappointment, not anger.

The replacement of Austin after 33 years as School Secretary soon after Dale arrived was not, Vokins considered, a coincidence. Though Austin was 'a fair man', he was also 'calculating and ruthless'. With Dale he knew he had 'met his match'. Nor can it have been coincidental that the Schools Committee instantly resolved that in future the Headmaster should be summoned to attend all committee, sub-committee and special subcommittee meetings. If these changes made for a more harmonious relationship between Dale and the Schools Committee, it did not eliminate friction. As in Pollard's time, the underlying cause was a struggle for power. Dale was still required to obtain formal permission for the sort of minor decisions which headmasters of most public schools would have taken in five seconds on their own authority. For example (two of dozens which could be given) in July 1930 he required permission to spend £16 on a duplicating machine for

One of a series of decorative certificates used by the School, this one signed by F. R. Dale in 1933.

An examination in the Great Hall, probably 1950s.

Jack Marsh, the longstanding English Master (sketch by Derek Fowler).

printing exam papers; and in March 1933 he needed permission to increase the chemical laboratory assistant's wages from £2 5s. to £2 10s. a week.

There was a bitter row in 1933 when the Boys' Representative Assembly asked for a School uniform. On the one hand the Chairman of the Schools Committee broke with precedent by announcing on Prize Day that this would be adopted, instead of letting the Headmaster make such an announcement; on the other hand the Schools Committee accused Dale of usurping its authority by writing to parents on the subject without its agreement. Dale coped successfully with such rebuffs, reacting not with obstinacy as Pollard had done, but, typically at that Prize Day, with 'a wry smile' (Vokins).

Though it was more for being the man he was than for things he did that boys and masters developed a passionate loyalty to Dale, he nevertheless made important changes. He quickly adopted streaming in the classics, modern and mathematics Sixth Forms, each of which he divided into parallel forms of boys of different abilities. This had had excellent results, he told the Schools Committee, and he now, in his first term, asked for an extra master in order to do the same with the science Sixth Form. At present 23 boys, 'some of whom were about University Scholarship standard while others have only just passed School Certificate' were being taught together.

If the School's masters admired Dale, he had almost as good an opinion of them. After just over a year (November 1930) he reported to the Schools

91

Committee 'There must of course be a distinction between those masters who are good and those who are very good indeed. But the latter are numerous, and the keenness with which the staff as a whole works is as remarkable as the loyalty with which they have worked together. I have no hesitation in recommending cordially that all of my colleagues be reappointed' (as all staff still had to be each year).

Among these masters Amis remembered in particular Jack Marsh ('sucking the earpiece of his glasses'), who would lend boys Auden and MacNeice to read; and the Revd C. J. Ellingham.

> At that time two years were allotted for preparation for the long-vanished School Certificate; Mr Ellingham was confident that his part of the syllabus could be covered in one, and illicitly used the other to see that we did not remain totally ignorant of classical music, painting and English poetry outside the official courses. Most of the poetry was of then recent years, though Mr Marsh's favourites were stopped short of. I had already discovered Housman for myself . . . but Mr Ellingham gave me a profound and necessary shock by announcing that Housman was his favourite poet – this from a very unequivocal Christian.

Boys also remembered the master often mentioned alongside Ellingham: Carey Oakley, head of classics (who, by the time he retired in 1957, had known the School as boy and master for 50 years). Liked and respected though he was they found him less outgoing and more 'bottled up' than Ellingham. He was noted for his spoonerisms, e.g. 'A scoop of boy trouts.' When Ellingham and Oakley retired Dale wrote that a headmaster's only difficulty when he had such men on his staff was not to overwork them.

The easy relationship between such masters and the boys is suggested by the summer camps (nothing to do with the OTC) which Sach and Vokins (then Marsh

The School in 1930, showing the building site next to it.

when Sach died) organised in the grounds of a girls' school at Goudhurst, Kent. Attendance was by invitation and in the nature of a reward. Sach's death at the age of 35 in 1936 after a short and totally unexpected illness, probably leukaemia, caused great grief to his many friends. Another Old Citizen was appointed to succeed him, Cyril Bond (1921–7, modern linguist), for many years Chairman of the commonroom until he retired in 1973.

Not surprisingly, the School with its 'vast agoraphobic playground filled with self-possessed boys in black coats and striped trousers' could seem alarming to new boys. Fear made Amis vomit on his first few mornings. But he

> quickly found that this was excessive . . . My fellows, I saw dimly, were drawn from a wide spectrum: accents varied from ones that discomforted me to ones that made me feel superior. But example at once taught me to put such attitudes aside. To be acceptable you had only to be amiable . . . I have never in my life known a community where factions of any kind were less in evidence, where differences of class, upbringing, income group and religion counted for so little. In particular, although perhaps 15 per cent of the boys were Jewish, not a single instance of even the mildest anti-Semitism came to my notice in the seven years I was a pupil there.

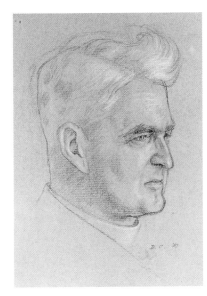

The Revd C. J. Ellingham, head of English (sketch by Derek Chittock).

It was not new that the boys of the School came from a 'wide spectrum' of society. Though the London County Council scholars introduced by Chilton when he arrived had ceased to come by 1920, in that year boys' parents were reported to be 22 per cent professional, 33 per cent wholesale or retail tradesmen and 37 per cent clerks or commercial agents. Furthermore, the moment Dale arrived he had obtained permission to readmit LCC minor scholars at the rate of 12 each September. He wanted, he explained to the Schools Committee, 'to brace up the standard of work, particularly in the middle class, by a regular intake of first-rate boys'. This and not social engineering had been his purpose and there is no doubt that he achieved the first as well as the second, the LCC scholars becoming for many years the School's academic backbone.

In the 1930s numerous school societies flourished, and the democratic structure was expanded with the formation of a Masters' Representative Assembly and a Boys' Representative Assembly. It was also a golden period for the Corps, with Certificate A as its central feature, guards of honour for the Lord Mayor and field days its special occasions. Most of the latter ended with only mock drama though not on the occasion on Aldershot Heath when Cadet Mark Jenner (1933–8) shot Cadet Baker. 'Baker had been firing his gun alongside my ear,' Jenner remembered. ' "Did you feel anything?" he said. "I certainly did," I replied, and placing the muzzle of my gun over his puttee, I fired my rifle. Blank cartridges, of course, do emit black powder and wadding. Baker looked at his puttee, which had a large hole in it the size of a half crown. He then fainted and was carried off the field. The OTC masters, not having warned the boys of the lethal properties of blank cartridges, were highly embarrassed and took little action against me.'

Carey Oakley, head of Classics, who knew the School as boy and master for 50 years (sketch by Derek Chittock).

For some parents the years of the Depression of the early 1930s were difficult. In May 1932 as many as 154 were in arrears with their fees. The Schools Committee was unsympathetic, regularly referring them to its solicitor and discussing whether the sons of those in debt should be allowed to continue at the School. By December 1933 only one parent still owed fees and in later years there were rarely more than a handful.

The staff had another reason for their loyalty to Dale. From his fourth term (December 1930) he campaigned steadily for an improvement to their salaries. By this time they had consulted him on the subject. His reply, according to Vokins, was 'I cannot support your claim, you have not asked for nearly enough.' He was waiting for the report of the School inspectors.

This was the second such report. The first, the result of an inspection in 1920, had spoken favourably of the School's classics teaching, but not of much else. The curriculum of the Modern Side was still 'not calculated to give boys a liberal education', and the Science Side was seriously handicapped by the lack of modern laboratories. Much had improved since them, but when the inspectors now came they found fault with something entirely outside the School's control: the noise, dust and dirt which engulfed playground and classrooms as a result of the replacing of the old Royal Hotel with Unilever House. They reported that 'the terrible noises . . . which are now filling a large number of rooms were in particular bound to have a serious effect on the efficiency of the modern language work.'

Unfortunate as this was, another part of their report gave Dale the opportunity he had needed. The inspectors pointed out:

(a) That the scales of salaries paid at the City of London School compared badly with those of London day schools of the same class.

(b) That the Heads of Departments received no additional remuneration for their work as such.

It was not, however, until June 1936 that the Schools Committee allowed Dale to prepare a new scale of salaries for assistant masters, and not until the autumn of the following year that improved salaries for all staff including heads of departments were finally agreed, back-dated to January 1937. The new salaries, which staff referred to as the Dale Scale, brought them much relief. The top salary was now Wilkinson's (£830 – an increase of £180) and there was now only one instead of three masters receiving less than £400. Though at the lower end the increases were not dramatic, they were made attractive by the inclusion of free education at the City of London Boys' or Girls' School for masters' offspring. Vokins remembered realising that he could now plan an entirely different education for his children.

This was an appropriate gesture in the School's centenary year, for if its success during its first hundred years can be attributed to any single cause this was the consistently high standard of its masters. A more visible celebration was the erection of a new set of classrooms and a swimming pool. When the Lord Mayor laid their foundation stone on 10 December 1936 the Magazine reported, 'On the edge of the muddy chasm in the northwest corner of the playground a small piece of new wall had somehow emerged, complete with canopy and platform, and above it hung the Foundation Stone, inscribed with the Lord Mayor's name and "The first year of King Edward VIII" (rather a near thing, we reflected, as we listened to the historic broadcast of 4 p.m.)' – the King's abdication speech.

The new block was a further extension of the 1927 extension north along John Carpenter Street – each known in turn as the New Wing. The swimming pool with plant, changing room and gallery occupied the lower part. This was a recognition

The centenary celebrations of the School in 1937 included a reception at Guildhall.

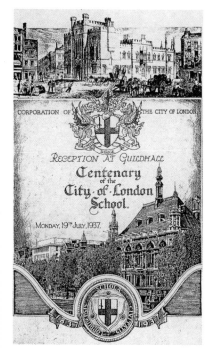

The new swimming pool (above left) *and exterior* (above) *of the New Wing built in 1937.*

of the School's many swimming successes (won in other pools) since Munro had founded a Swimming Club in 1901. Above were five new classrooms, one for each Sixth Form apart from Science, and above again a biology laboratory and new art/music room. About the complete building the Magazine wrote, 'whatever the cynics muttered about the new building looking like a factory outside, the interior of the bath is quite a thing of beauty with its soft colours and smooth lines'.

A service of thanksgiving at St Paul's on 2 March 1937 was the first official occasion of the centenary year. A centenary dinner for staff followed in April and in May a tea at Guildhall for pupils of the boys' and girls' schools. 'As we sat waiting for the Lord Mayor, a band played martial and patriotic tunes, to which all responded as inclination or a sense of duty moved them, and the heat permitted. The Lord Mayor came, and marched through the dignitaries, who must have found their uniforms very hot indeed. We then cheered for some time; it is strange that emotion is gauged by noise.'

Presently 'an astounding amount of excellent food was eaten, and a prodigious quantity of tea and lemonade drunk.' In sum it was 'one of the great events in the School's history; an afternoon which everybody enjoyed in some measure, not least those who assured themselves of their superiority by an amused contempt for such simple-minded pleasure.'

In 1937 George VI was crowned king, an event which gave the whole year a celebratory flavour. The following year the outside world began to impinge less agreeably on the School, and plans were made in case of war for it to be evacuated to South Wales. After the supposed peace arranged between Chamberlain and Hitler at the end of September 1938 this idea was abandoned, but during the autumn a new arrangement was made: the School would go to Marlborough College.

Marlborough had been one of the first of the new boarding schools of the 1840s, opening just six years after the City of London School had opened in Milk Street, particularly designed to offer cheap boarding education to the sons of Anglican parsons. Its central mansion had been one of the Duke of Somerset's several country mansions before becoming a coaching inn. Around this Edward Blore,

The School evacuated to Marlborough College during the War. City of London boys in the Court in 1940 (above)*, and* (below) *in the library there.*

'the cheap architect', had erected prison-like school buildings of red brick but nevertheless produced a front courtyard of pleasing character. As for the college's setting, in downland on the western outskirts of the town with its own mini-Silbury Hill behind the dining hall, this could hardly have been more delightful. After an early revolution it had become one of the best-regarded English public schools, and under George Turner, the Master since 1926, had been ahead in civilising itself, for example by abolishing personal fagging.

It was with Turner that Dale had made the evacuation agreement. He and Turner were men of a similar rectitude, both with distinguished war records. Turner was said to have captured a batch of German prisoners single-handed by telling them to 'Come along with me'. These two trusted each other – Dale later wrote about Turner 'our list of benefactors holds no greater name' – and it was unfortunate that within six months of the agreement Turner had been succeeded by a less experienced Master, F. M. Heywood.

The majority of the School set out for Marlborough by train on 1 September 1939, each boy carrying a bag of emergency rations and his gas mask in its little cardboard box. All went well till they reached Ealing Broadway where they were put into a train which, they discovered, was bound non-stop for the far West Country. As it ran through Reading, however, the economics master, Charles Wilmot, flung out a message wrapped in a CLS towel which was received by a member of the Great Western Railway staff who managed to have the train halted at Savernake, the station for Marlborough.

The arrangement with the college did not include sleeping accommodation and in order to persuade the Mayor of Marlborough to provide billets in the town,

Turner had had to write to him. 'From the point of view of the town, I think that there may be a good deal to be said for such an arrangement. The City of London School boys are decently brought up and trained in some degree of responsibility. They would be much less inconvenient lodgers than, for instance, a large number of small children from the poorest districts of London.' The Mayor had been persuaded but in September 1939 many of the billets were still occupied by holiday makers, soldiers and women working for the Ministry of Health, so for the first night about 120 boys slept in the Marlborough gymnasium (on camp beds wisely stockpiled by the Schools Committee), and during the next few days lived in local barns. In this period Amis remembered that 'I ate about twenty tins of sweetened condensed milk, the discarded residue of my companions' train rations.'

In the three weeks before the Marlborough term began the City of London School boys learned their way around the Marlborough buildings and grounds, and practised the complicated timetable which was to enable the two schools to share these. Basically, the City of London School boys did lessons while the Marlborough boys played games, and vice versa. For the London boys this meant an 8 a.m. class followed by breakfast then two periods of games. Next came two classes from 12.30 to 2, followed by lunch. In the afternoons there were further alternating periods of games and lessons.

'We enjoyed the period before breakfast,' Dale wrote (using, perhaps, the royal 'we'), 'boys were in excellent form for the two pre-lunch periods . . . and even the long afternoons were tolerable.'

Inevitably there were difficulties. Dale at first was given no study and had to be found one in what he described as 'an affair called the Old Music School'. (It was in the cellar of the Old Music School that boys of the City of London School were found keeping themselves warm round a Tortoise stove by feeding it with Marlborough's early historical records.) Marlborough's kitchen staff had to be 'reinforced by one collected with great difficulty by ourselves' (Magazine). The Marlborough authorities reported more frankly that the promised City of London School kitchen staff never arrived. 'Some Marlborough masters,' Dale wrote, 'did not see their opportunity as Mr Turner had seen it.' (Interestingly, one of those he picked out for helpfulness was the mathematics master, Robson, whose career at Marlborough ended six years later in an attempt to have Heywood dismissed.)

Some London boys found that first winter a rough experience. Richard Heron (1935–40) was billeted in the town

> under the care of an elderly couple who to a teenager seemed positively ancient. Facilities were basic – an outside toilet and a weekly bath in a tin tub filled with water from a boiling copper. They were very kind. I still recall with almost fondness the old man sitting before the permanent kitchen range sucking his pipe and spitting into the fire. That winter was blessed with appalling weather when the whole of Marlborough was one sheet of ice. My mother sent me my skates which were great for skating down the High Street and for playing ice hockey on the College pool, much to the fury of their authorities. The inevitable happened with an epidemic of German measles accompanied by flu. I fell to the latter and was laid in the gym together with hundreds of others as the Marlborough boys had filled their sanatorium . . . My neighbour on the gym floor became delirious,

Damage to the north end of the playground and the swimming pool, 1944.

465 to 226, those at the rump which remained in Highgate rose steadily. By Easter 1944 numbers at the City of London School had fallen from 700 to 430, and since London now seemed safer it decided to bring itself back to the Embankment.

Though some raids were expected and the School prepared itself in case these occurred in daytime (there was a shelter in the basement, the cloakroom was sandbagged and four shelters of concrete blocks were built in the tuckshop and dining room) it did not expect what began to happen on the night of 15–16 June. By the time boys arrived at the School next morning there had still been no 'All Clear'. 'Boys went down into shelter,' Turnu Severin (probably Dale) wrote, 'and stories of the night were exchanged. "They came over regularly every quarter of an hour." "They are jet-propelled things – you can see a fiery tail." "They say there are no pilots on them – they just cut out and drop".'

Nine months of flying bomb and V2-rocket attacks followed. The School was lucky; no boy was killed or seriously hurt, and it suffered no structural damage, but its work was much disrupted. That first Monday (18 June) 'A flying bomb had just passed low over the building and dropped on the Law Courts.' Everyone was sent home for a week. Dale's chief concern was to enable senior boys to take their summer external exams, and when it became clear that this could not be done at the School he asked Marlborough to receive a visiting party of 170 for the purpose, but the request was refused. Eventually boys took their Higher Certificate papers in the secure basement of Unilever House, and their School Certificate papers in Guildhall Crypt. On 19 July, while these boys were making their way to Guildhall one bomb fell on Cannon Street and another in Old Jewry, with the result that they arrived 'dusty and shaken' – except for one who was 'missing all morning' and found to have been digging out casualties.

During Dale's final five years (1945–50), when food was still rationed and trams still ran along the Embankment, the School shared in the country's generally dilapidated condition. The damaged swimming baths, for example, were not usable again until 1949. Harry Lee-Uff, who arrived to teach classics in 1947, remembered that the front part of the School was magnificent but the back parts seemed squalid. Harry Law-Robertson, who arrived the same year to become head of Modern Languages, wrote, 'In those days there were still coal fires in the older parts of the School and I well remember "Gus", the second porter, pushing the coal trolley along the corridor.' (Until central heating was installed in 1954 it was the duty of a class's fire monitor each morning to bring from the boiler room a shovel of red-hot coals to start the open fire.) Before applying for the job Law-Robertson had taken the precaution of paying the School an uninvited visit, when, 'totally unchallenged', he had 'wandered through the classrooms and been duly impressed by the quality of the Library in the Modern Language Section. That we were less than security conscious in those days, I am reminded by the appearance in my classroom of a character brandishing a poker. With the help of Sidney, the head porter, we managed to persuade him to leave quietly.'

But in one way the returned School became at once embarrassingly successful. Though the 430 boys who left Marlborough had become 499 when they reassembled a month later in London these did not provide the basis for the number of academic successes which Dale hoped it would soon again be winning and he allowed it to expand so rapidly that by 1948 its numbers had risen to almost exactly 850. This was too many – classes were being held in corridors – and when Dale agreed that year to stay a final two years he considered it a duty to his successor to eliminate some boys who had been admitted 'without sufficient sifting'. Though he 'did this best to be fair' (Vokins) this inevitably caused disappointment to certain parents.

Meanwhile on 6 November 1947 the Lord Mayor opened an afternoon of demonstrations and exhibits at the School to celebrate the hundredth anniversary of its start of science teaching. The exhibits were displayed in 22 laboratories and science classrooms. There were now 168 boys on the School's Science Side and ten science masters. In a review of the occasion R. H. Dyball, head of science, gave particular credit to his predecessor, G. H. J. Adlam, head of science from 1912 to 1944, who had founded and edited the *School Science Review*, so gaining recognition for the quality of science teaching at the School.

In these post-war years some masters thought that Dale became somewhat easygoing. Lee-Uff remembered finding him in his study doing *The Times* crossword. When he had listened to Lee-Uff's problem he said only, 'You handle it,' and returned to *The Times*. But 'he always knew what was going on in the School and where if anywhere there was a problem'. Similarly, Law-Robertson remembered,

> [H]e was a man of few words. On seeking his advice . . . he would spend a moment looking out of the window at the swans on the Thames before replying 'Yes, I expect that will be in order.' On receiving a tediously long and irate letter from a woman travelling on the Northern Underground, who had been offended at not being offered a seat by a City of London

Boxing at the school, 1947.

Schoolboy (easily recognisable then by his School cap and blazer) he replied . . . 'Dear Madam, I dare say you're right.'

But such economy had always been Dale's style, and had never prevented him attracting, as he did to the end, the virtually unanimous loyalty of his staff and admiration of the boys. When he retired he was 67, older than any previous serving Headmaster, but he continued to be actively involved in educational matters. In 1949 he had been given an honorary MA by London University, and in 1950 he received an OBE. Without doubt he will be seen as the School's great twentieth-century Headmaster.

The School in 1946, as sketched by Peter Jones (CLS 1938–46).

10

Barton and Earnest Endeavour

1950~1965

D R ARTHUR BARTON – aged 50, for the last eleven years Headmaster of King Edward VII School, Sheffield – came to the City of London School with more various qualifications than any previous Headmaster. Most interestingly, he was the first to be a scientist: his London University Ph.D. had been on radioactivity, he had been Supervisor of Physics at Trinity and other Cambridge Colleges where he was a demonstrator at the Cavendish when Rutherford first split the atom, and for 14 years had been chief physics master at Repton School. He had also written textbooks on Heat and Light. Most curiously he was an internationally recognised soccer referee, performing at the Olympic Games and at the FA Amateur Cup Final; when he came to the School he soon learned to referee Rugby. According to Gordon Nobbs (known to the boys by his other name, Cyril), Second Master from 1928 to 1968 and often considered to have been as influential as the Headmasters he served under, Barton was 'passionately fair minded . . . I have often wondered whether this is an innate quality which found an outlet in refereeing or whether refereeing developed it in him.' Barton's other sport was rock climbing. In August he would take parties of boys to climb in Switzerland.

Despite his many good qualities, some staff found his commitment to Low Church Christianity unsympathetic. (In Sheffield he had been a member of the Diocesan Ordination Candidates Committee.) 'He was rarely seen to laugh,' Law-Robertson remembered, 'or even smile, and took life as seriously as he did his post-luncheon walk along the Thames Embankment. I still recall his look of disapproval when the attractive wife of the art master, at an after-dinner School reception, lit a cheroot.'

Denis Moore, who joined the staff the same year as Barton and was to succeed Nobbs as Second Master, admitted Barton's lack of a sense of humour, typified by an observation at one assembly: 'If you take exercise when young your body will last you the rest of your life.' But on the whole his verdict was more favourable: Barton was 'an authoritarian of the old school. His two main criteria were academic

Dr Arthur Barton, Headmaster 1950–1965.

excellence and success in games.' Since the 1850s many a great headmaster has had precisely these aims.

Barton was a sound if uninspiring teacher, spending more time in the classroom than most modern headmasters. His method was to expound rather than to encourage discussion, indeed his 'passion for imparting precise information' was part of his character. Nobbs remembered being asked by Barton to post some books: 'Go to the porter, ask him for brown paper and string, get the books from the form master and make up a parcel. The porters will post it for you.' Not surprisingly, his main subject was physics, but he would also during one term a year lecture to the 150 non-science Sixth Form boys on 'Science and Religion', with the aim of introducing them to concepts like the expanding universe and relativity. And he would take confirmation classes, lecturing in particular on the 7th Commandment ('Thou shalt not commit adultery') which in effect was the sort of sex talk traditionally given as preparation for confirmation to embarrassed

View of the School from the other side of the river, 1950s, with Sion College on the left and Unilever House on the right.

and already well-informed public school boys. Ellingham took the other Commandments.

In addition Barton would visit classes throughout the School. Then, as always, the boys would stand for the Headmaster, but Barton would only let them sit as he remembered each of their names, a process which might keep some of them on their feet for ten minutes. These failures in what he considered his duty 'were more painful to him than to the boys' (Ian Cameron Black, 1949–57).

Barton at once introduced important changes to the structure of the middle school (Forms Three, Four and Five). In Dale's time each of these had been divided into classical, modern and science classes. As a result boys were having to specialise from about the age of 13. Apart from the undesirability of narrowing their education so early, this meant that boys from the classical and modern Fifth Forms who wished to change to science in the Sixth Form had to spend an extra year there learning the elementary science they did not know. It was also found that boys who

1950s classroom (above) *and view of the playground* (above right).

R. H. Dyball OBE, Senior Science Master, who founded the Scientific Society (sketch by Derek Fowler).

had done much science in the middle school had lost some of their enthusiasm for the subject by the time they reached the Sixth. Such arguments for a change seem as valid today as in 1950, but others Barton used seem curiously of their time. Under the old arrangement, he explained, the clever boys of the School were divided among the three different Sides, and since there was a limited number of them, they had to be taught in classes largely composed of less clever boys. This meant that bright boys were held back, dim boys were made to feel dimmer and masters had to teach mixed-ability classes which they found discouraging and difficult. He now created five classes at each level, all to study a broad range of subjects, but to be made up of boys divided according to their cleverness.

Throughout his time Barton, like his predecessors, was supported by an able and committed staff. In the commonroom Moore remembered that there was virtually no friction between older and younger members, and 'we were always able to harbour – and often to learn from, one or two eccentrics'. Among these was the science master, J. P. Stephenson, known as Steve to fellow masters and to boys (whom he would similarly call by their first names). Sometimes Stephenson was to be found lying flat on his back on the commonroom floor relaxing after a lesson. He would also lie on his back on his classroom bench to suggest the effect of his weight applied over a wide area. In this position he once became aware that his boys were standing, realised that the Headmaster had arrived and got quickly off the bench, landing on one of the Headmaster's feet. Undismayed, he told the class that this was an excellent demonstration of the much greater effect of the same weight applied at a single point.

It was, of course, easier in the 1950s to gain a reputation for eccentricity, when conformity of dress, for example, was strictly enforced. Masters came in bowler hats or trilbys which they were expected to wear until they reached the commonroom, and all wore suits, usually with waistcoats. Stephenson was anyway no buffoon but a teacher of reputation. He had a remarkable skill in making physics apparatus out of ordinary materials, and several of his inventions (the Ray Box, the Ripple Tank, the Coil and Channel Apparatus) were widely used in other countries. For UNESCO he wrote *Source Book of Science Teaching in War-Devastated Countries*, which was translated into ten languages. In 1949 he became chairman of the Science Masters' Association.

Other masters who took advantage of the School's London location to involve themselves in national bodies were R. H. Dyball, an active member of the same association, Nobbs and J. W. Hunt, who became Chairmen of the mathematics and history committees respectively of the Ministry of Education's 1965 Schools Council.

Valuable contact of another kind with the educational world was provided by the postgraduate students sent to the School for their teaching practice by Oxford, Cambridge, King's College London, Goldsmith's College and the Institute of Education. Some of these students later returned to become permanent members of the staff, and all brought with them current ideas about teaching and teacher training.

As so often, some members of staff were best remembered for activities other than the teaching of their subjects. These included Hector Starr, who from 1925 onwards helped to make swimming a major sport at the School, Jack Wheeler who did the same for fencing, and above all the classics and English master, G. Irwin Carruthers, who finally retired in 1964 after 36 years at the School without a single absence for illness. He was the School's Rugby coach for 12 years and it was said that no masters' team of any sort ever played without him. His wider interests included singing, playing the violin or viola in the School orchestra, brewing mead, mending zip-fasteners, flint-knapping, sketching, painting and writing light verse. Throughout his time he was involved in the production (and sometimes the writing) of School plays.

G. Irwin-Carruthers, English and Classics master (sketch by Derek Fowler).

John Wray, Director of Music, conducting hymn practice in the 1950s.

More important for his influence on School drama was Geoffrey Clark, who for 21 years (1947–67) staged plays in the theatre of Guildhall School of Music and Drama.

He had a gift [Lee-Uff remembered] for eliciting exceptionally good performances from his boy actors but, perhaps more important, he succeeded in welding together a company where each individual, from leading actor to callboy, was convinced of his responsibility as a member of the team. It always seemed to me it was an experience of much greater importance for the individual than being a member of a successful cricket XI or rugger XV.

During Barton's time there was a significant change in the make-up of the commonroom. When he arrived the youngest master was 33, a result of the Schools Committee's policy of only appointing masters with three or four years' experience, and of the war which had delayed many from obtaining this. When Barton left there were 14 masters under 30.

The appointment of John Wray as Director of Music was one of Barton's most successful. Music at the School had only developed modestly since the efforts made by Chilton and the School Society in the 1920s to encourage it. A Director of Music had been appointed, a School choir formed and singing lessons introduced in the Junior School, but in 1950 when Barton arrived the then Director was a gentleman who (in the words of Terry Heard, 1953–9) 'seemed to favour the teaching of music by numbers, without the inconvenience of actually making any sound.' When Barton asked him to form a school orchestra he replied that he was too busy. A notice from the Headmaster then appeared on the commonroom board announcing that 'the Director of Music has resigned because of pressure of other commitments.' This was the first he knew of it but he went.

Above: *The New Junior School, 1956, also containing a gymnasium, woodwork room and art room.* Below: *Sixth Form physical training in the gym* (Illustrated London News, *1959*).

Wray ('cherubic, rotund, slightly balding') who was then appointed had his problems with Barton, who once sent him home because the trousers and jacket of the suit he was wearing did not match. Another confrontation concerned a second-hand grand piano which the Corporation had given the School to celebrate the 1953 Coronation. This instrument was still due to be officially presented at an inaugural recital by Frank Lafitte (1914–15) when the Great Hall's organ failed (as it quite often did). Wray therefore told Barton that he would play the Assembly hymn on the new piano. 'Oh, but you can't do that,' Barton replied. 'It hasn't been inaugurated.' Only when Wray pointed out that there was no other functioning instrument and after carefully considering the issue did Barton deliver his judgement: 'All right – but don't play too loud.' From 1950 onwards, however, it was Wray, generally with Barton's less qualified support, who began to create at the School the sort of outstanding music department which it has today.

On 27 June 1956 the most significant new School building of Barton's time was opened by the Lord Mayor. It stood at the Tudor Street end of the School's playground, on the site of a block of bombed offices and was generally called the new Junior School, but it also contained a new gymnasium and fencing salle, a scout room, an art room and a woodwork room. The Lord Mayor hoped that the Headmaster 'would not hesitate to ask the Guild of Carpenters for any tools, wood or technical help that the School needed' for the last of these.

In November the following year the School Mission celebrated its fiftieth anniversary, but with a lavishness which proved fatal, finally convincing boys that the parishioners of St Barnabas, Mitcham, were no more in need of charity than most of their own parents. From 1958 the School's contributions to St Barnabas were progressively eliminated and instead an annual charity, which the boys selected, was supported. Over the previous three years the School's annual contribution to St Barnabas had averaged £150. The sums collected for the chosen charity rose from £2,548 in 1967 to a record £48,000 in 1987 (for the Joseph Patrick Memorial Trust). Since then they have never fallen below £23,000, the charities supported including Guide Dogs for the Blind, the Cystic Fibrosis Research Trust and Save the Children.

To Cameron Black the most memorable feature of the School in his time was its summer camps. These had been revived after the war by M. F. (Rockie) Cornish, but now commonly took place abroad. For two and a half weeks Cornish, with the help of some four other masters and a few Old Citizens, would take as many as 130 boys to the Massif Central, the Alps, the Tyrol or some other place where he had arranged with a farmer to use a field or orchard. Huge amounts of food (including daily porridge and custard for stewed fruit) had to be cooked in billy cans over Primuses or open fires. The only rules were 'No smoking or drinking in public', but Black never remembers any misbehaviour – wisely the chosen sites would be not less than a couple of miles from any town or village.

Looking back on Barton as his Headmaster, Black considered that his intentions were never less than worthy but that he had serious disadvantages, the chief of these that he did not know how to communicate. As a result boys feared him. He also, in Black's opinion, lacked any strong personal feeling for the arts.

On the other hand he knew what he ought to encourage. His end-of-term homily, time after time, told boys to use the holidays for reading some good books, visiting some good exhibitions, seeing some good plays and films. Increasingly, Black came to look back on him as 'a damned good headmaster'.

Gordon Nobbs, Second Master 1928–1968.

Summer camp, 1955. The shot on the left appeared in the Magazine under the title 'The Call of the Inner Man'.

Athletic success under Dr Barton.
Above: *Tennis, 1957.* Top: *Horace Brearley, who played cricket for Yorkshire and Middlesex, coaching a boy.* Top right: *The Beaufoy Rowing Club, 1955.*

Certainly by the time Barton retired in 1965 he could claim that his two main aims for the School – academic and athletic success – were being well fulfilled. That year boys won 14 scholarships and 20 other places at Oxbridge, and 30 more at other universities or medical schools. The tennis and swimming teams had won all their 20 school matches, the tennis team being only defeated in the final of the Glanville Cup. Michael Brearley (1952–60), son of the mathematics master and school cricket coach, Horace Brearley, had of course been the outstanding cricketer, later to captain England when they won the Ashes in 1977, 1978/9 and 1981. Another had been M. J. Edmonds (1957–65), who had scored 694 runs in his last season including 129 against the MCC. Edmonds also partnered C. S. Hampton (1954–64) when they were runners-up in the Public Schools Eton Fives Championship. And the School had had a remarkable chess player, William Hartston (1958–65), who became British Chess Champion in 1973 and 1975.

Successful as Barton's headship had on the whole been, he was lucky to retire when he did. At his first Prize Day he had urged every boy to be 'willing to give himself to and lose himself in the School, and by so doing' to find himself – not a fashionable view in the years of student protest which were soon to follow.

11

Boyes – Radical Planner
1965~1984

R ESPECTED BARTON MAY HAVE BEEN and soundly he undoubtedly managed
the School, but certain masters never warmed to him. Law-Robertson
remembered that when his successor, James Boyes, arrived 'it was almost
like a Restoration after a Cromwellian autocracy . . . The whole atmosphere of the
School became more happy and relaxed.' Other contrasts were to follow. Barton's
15 years had been relatively free of drama and change, but the opposite was to be
the case during Boyes' 19 years.

Boyes, who arrived for the autumn term of 1965, was both a scholar and a
sportsman. Educated at Rugby (where he later also taught), he had taken a history
degree at Cambridge followed by an economics and politics MA at Yale. Most
recently he had been Director of Studies at the RAF College, Cranwell. At Rugby
he had been captain of rugger, cricket and rackets, at Cambridge he had played
rugger for the university and he was also a player of tennis and squash, a swimmer
and a yachtsman. As important as any of these qualifications, in the opinion of
Lee-Uff, was that he was a man with 'bags of humanity'.

From the start Boyes' central preoccupation was the moving of the School to a
new site. This was by no means the first time such an idea had been considered. In
1930 an unknown bidder (probably Unilever) had offered to buy the
Embankment site. The Schools Committee had taken the offer seriously. It needed
to move the girls' school and when Merchant Taylors', about to move to
Northwood, offered its Holborn site, considered using this for both boys' and girls'
schools. Finally in 1932 the Committee rejected the idea as it did more quickly
another in 1936 which came with the option of a new site at White City. Twenty
years later a plan to move to the Barbican was also rejected, but the need to move
from a building which seemed ever more antiquated was underlined by the
Blackfriars Bridgehead Improvement Scheme, agreed in 1960, opened in 1967,
which reduced the land separating the School from Embankment traffic. At first
the question was still whether or not to move, but even when a move had been
agreed the more difficult question of where to go remained.

*James Boyes, Headmaster
1965–1984.*

A hundred years after the first London schools had started to leave for the sub-urbs or the country there were still staff and members of the Schools Committee who thought this was the right thing to do, urging as their predecessors had done that the new School could then be sited close to its playing fields. Others success-fully argued that if the School moved from the City it would no longer be able to attract boys from all parts of London as it had for more than a hundred years, and that anyway there was now less enthusiasm in the upper school for games like rugby and cricket which needed playing fields.

Fortunately an ideal London site was about to become available, on the oppo-site (east) side of Blackfriars Bridge between the river and Queen Victoria Street, for which redevelopment plans were still incomplete though they had been under discussion for 25 years. It was a move to this site which the Chairman of the Schools Committee, Alec Coulson, proposed on 10 July 1969 and to which the Court of Common Council agreed. The saga of the move had barely begun. That October Boyes told his Prize Day audience that it might be 'five years or so' before the new School was ready. He was too optimistic by 13 years.

The City Architect, Stuart Murphy (1944–50), had in fact been preparing plans for the now agreed site since 1967, and already had them ready in outline. He now worked on the details, but because of problems with planning permission and roads these took him a further two and a half years. The whole plan was then seen to be too ambitious. 'We designed a palace of a school,' Boyes said. 'The sports hall would have rivalled the Crystal Palace.' Such a school would have been impossibly expen-sive to run, and the architect was asked to produce a more modest scheme.

A further year and a half passed before, in May 1973, this was ready, but there was now unfortunately a boom in the building industry so that it was impossible to obtain tenders which would have been covered by the sale of the old School; it was on this that the plan depended. Still worse, a year later the Government curbed local authority spending and passed the Community Land Act which threatened the value of the old School and its site.

There was now a five-year interval before building contractors began to make offers to build the new School in return for the old Embankment site. First came

Opposite page: The Hall, looking towards the organ.

Site of the new School, looking east.

112

The Tuck
the School
admired that
for all sorts o
without any
hope compos
about to star

By 1968
take the form
ferred to the
two hundred
a part or worl
middle schoo
being a memo
of English an

Boyes was
sidered that tl
advantage of
formed a corp
had been succe
as 'a flamboya
space, more sta
to grant. He i
the number of
arships and wo
fine new Wall
Marlborough,
to succeed him

By then the
appear three ti
issues the cont

Wimpey, but the Corporation turned down its offer (mistakenly in Boyes' later opinion). Next came Trafalgar House, but in return for building the new school it wanted not only the old School but Guildhall School of Music and the Girls' School sites as well. The Corporation, however, was about to accept this offer when Guildhall School was made a listed building and could therefore not be demolished. Trafalgar House persisted, but now required the School to move into the semi-derelict former Music School and Girls' School during the two or three years when the new School was being built so that it could develop the old site. Reluctantly the Corporation would have accepted this new offer but in 1982 Trafalgar House withdrew from the deal because it could not finance it.

As a result of all this it was not until 1984, Boyes' last year, that the Corporation, which had recently sold its Billingsgate Fish Market site, decided to finance the new School itself. 'For most of my 19 years,' Boyes said at that year's Prize Day, 'we seem to have been talking about the new School; consulting, drawing plans, altering plans, having encouragements followed by setbacks, hoping, being disappointed, hoping again. Now we are really on the way.'

Though the new building had been Boyes' central preoccupation, it had not been his only one. These years had included what he called 'the period of "Ferment",' when the 1968 student riots in Paris had been followed by sit-ins, demonstrations and the occupation of staff offices at British universities, their underlying aim the dismantling of 'the repressive, authoritarian and capitalist system' under which all educational establishments functioned. Ideas of this sort were spread by a so-called Schools' Student Union, and reached boys of the City of London School in the form of leaflets handed them on their way to school.

Boyes remembered that they were on the whole thought 'rather comic', but he was nevertheless approached by an informal Sixth Form committee which asked for various reforms, 'some of which would have been anathema both to the board of Governors and to the majority of parents. This was a dilemma for the Headmaster,' he continued. 'To use the heavy hand of authority and veto everything would have been counter-productive and disillusioning; but how to channel the activists' enthusiasm away from patently disastrous policies?' He hit upon the answer: *committees*. At his suggestion, four separate committees were set up, chairmen and secretaries appointed, minutes to be kept, and each committee to present a full written report in three months' time. Thus, the curriculum committee were presented with a copy of the massive school timetable, and asked to include in their report a detailed revision of the timetable in order to incorporate the radical proposals they had in mind. The committee met five or six times, wrestling with the interlocking intricacies of timetabling the academic work of a large school, and eventually gave up in despair. Even less fortunate was the finance committee. Asking to know how the School's revenue was spent with a view to reform, they were provided with a copy of the City Corporation's annual accounts. In those days, the School's income and expenditure was mixed up in the accounts under various headings along with the Corporation's many other commitments; and to anyone unacquainted with the ways of the Chamberlain's office the massive tome of the annual accounts was a formidable maze. 'The poor finance committee also gave up the struggle after several weeks. In fact none of the four committees ever presented its final report; but no one could say that they were not given a chance.'

Opposite page: The courtyard (above), and (below) the playground seen from the roof of the junior wing.

Denis Moore, Second Master 1968–1980 (sketch by Derek Fowler).

113

music. In March the following year the three City schools gave their first joint concert at the Barbican.

Of the many outstanding masters of Hammond's time he picked out inevitably his Second Master, Terry Heard, for special mention, and also Jonathan Keates, novelist, biographer of Stendhal, Handel and Purcell, and Lionel Knight, head of history, who together formed 'the planks of the intellectual life of the School'. To these he added Colin Ranger, Chairman of the Common Room, head of science.

When Hammond left the School after only six years there were inevitably some who wondered why. He admits that there was one way in which he found his position difficult: unlike virtually every other public school, the City of London School was owned by its local authority, and he was therefore responsible to two layers of management. The top layer (the City Corporation) was inclined to treat the School like its other departments and apply to it restraining regulations which were proper to those departments responsible for spending taxpayers' money, but not appropriate or necessary for the School which was quite a different sort of organisation and which to a large extent funded itself. It applied these restraints chiefly through its Establishment and its Policy and Resources Committees, which might veto decisions on which the Headmaster and the School's Governing Body had agreed.

The most controversial example of this concerned a house for the Headmaster. Hammond was anxious that he should be given one, not for himself but because one should automatically go with the job, as it did with the headmastership of virtually all similar schools. He had reached agreement with the Governing Body that this was right, and a plan had been accepted to build a Headmaster's flat on the roof of the new school when this was vetoed by the Corporation's Policy and Resources Committee, on the grounds that none of the Corporation's other department heads were given houses.

But Hammond firmly denies that this or any other difficulty with the Corporation was the reason for his leaving the School, pointing out that if he had stayed, like all but one previous City of London School Headmasters, until he reached retiring age he would have been there for 26 years, something which would not have been good for the School; and that although he would have liked to stay longer, when the opportunity to apply for the headmastership of Tonbridge School occurred, he could not afford to miss it. Nor had he any complaints about his direct employers, the School's Governing Body, which gave him steady support.

In the same farewell article, Keates wrote 'People who shake institutions by the scruff of the neck must not expect to endear themselves universally, and there was never much evidence that Martin Hammond, with all his operational acumen and iron determination, cared much about this.' Keates continued, 'If Martin Hammond set his mark upon CLS, then there can be no doubt that CLS in its turn took him somewhat by surprise.' Hammond's final comment on the School suggests something similar. It was a place of 'continuously humming electricity which kept us all on our toes'.

Opposite page: The Concourse, connecting the main staircase and the Courtyard. The statue of John Carpenter is on the wall to the left.

The sundial presented by the John Carpenter Club in 1987, with a plinth made from remains of a Roman building found during excavations under the Sports Wing. The Latin inscription, in the form of iambic pentameters, by Martin Hammond, reads:

Nos veteres fecere: aetas oblita, refecit
Tu tamen aetatis sis memor: hora fugit

[The ancients made us: time forgot us, but has restored us.
You should remember time: the hour is passing.]

The model rail... the many Schoo... the new School...

13

Today and Tomorrow
1990~1995

BRYAN BASS, HAMMOND'S SUCCESSOR, came from Hymers College, Hull, where he had been headmaster for seven years, but it was Manchester Grammar School where he had spent the previous 12 years, becoming head of its modern side, on which he based his expectations of the character of the City of London School. Hymers had been the only important independent school in Hull, and therefore a community school with a local catchment area. Manchester Grammar School boys had come from all over a vast conurbation. The largely urban boys of the City of London School would also, he guessed, be thrustingly anarchic and imbued with a healthy restlessness. He was in no sense disappointed. A school, he believed, cannot stand still. If it becomes complacent there is only one way for it to go: down. This was not likely to happen at the City of London School where staff and boys alike were 'always looking for new things to become and do'. The discomforts of this restlessness were far out-weighed by its usefulness.

His only surprise was the multi-racial character of the School, which by the 1990s included 35 per cent Jewish boys and 12 per cent Hindu or Muslim boys; but far from finding this a problem he believed it to be a great asset, bringing to the School many exceptionally talented pupils and teaching to all a broadminded-ness which boys in other schools had less opportunity to learn.

Bass also came with firm ideas about that perennial subject of educational debate: streaming. He was against it. No boy, he believed, should perceive that he is perceived to be of lesser value. Putting a boy into a lower stream did exactly this. His first and he considered most important reform was finally to abolish what remained after his two predecessors had already modified Barton's streaming arrangements. Boys in the middle school would be divided as before into two-language and three-language classes, but these classes would be entirely unstreamed. Even 'setting' for boys with special talents was preserved only for French and mathematics. There was opposition, he admitted, but he believed that almost all staff now approved of the change.

Opposite page: *The Design and Technology Centre, built 1991.*

Bryan Bass, Headmaster 1990–1995.

The teaching staff in 1995.

CHAPTER HEADPIECES

The headpieces to the Chapters are taken from contemporary School literature, or from the coats of arms of the City of London as they were close to the date of the Chapter. The exact dates and sources are as follows: Chapter 1, pre-1600, Guildhall Library; Chapter 2, 1560, Guildhall Library; Chapter 3, 1820, Guildhall Library; Chapter 4, 1840, School annual statement of accounts; Chapter 5, 1860, School common council report; Chapter 6, 1870, Guildhall Library; Chapter 7, 1905, Souvenir of the Saturday Club; Chapter 8, 1913, School Magazine; Chapter 9, 1937, Centenary thanksgiving service invitation card; Chapter 10, 1964, School Magazine; Chapter 11, 1970, School Magazine; Chapter 12, 1987, Official opening of the new School program; Chapter 13, undated, Guildhall Library.

The coat of arms in Chapter 1 is described as follows: *The Armorial Atchievments of the most Opulent City London are Argent, a Cross gules, on ye 1st quarter a sword (by some falsly called yt of St Paul, by others ye Dagger of St William Walworth, but I take it to represent yt) of Justice, of ye 2nd ye Crest on a helmet and Tors, a Dragons Wing expanced & erected of ye first bearing ye Cross of St George. Supporters 2 dragons Segreiant, Coloured, and their Wings Charged as ye Crest.*

Selected List of Old Citizens

VEN E. W. EMERY (1837-1843), Archdeacon of Ely and founder of the Church Congress

SIR WILLIAM HUGGINS, LL.D, FRS (1837–1839), KCB., OM, developed modern astronomy by using spectroscopy and photography; proved the gaseous nature of nebulae; President of the Royal Society from 1900 to 1905, and of the British Association in 1891

C. W. C. HUTTON (1837), Sheriff of the City of London

GEORGE SMITH (1837-1838), doyen of 19th century English publishers and friend of Darwin, Ruskin, Charlotte Bronte, Thackeray, George Eliot, Browning, founder of the *Cornhill Magazine* and the *Pall Mall Gazette,* and of the *Dictionary of National Biography* (edited by Sidney Lee, q.v.)

SIR HARRY SMITH PARKES, GCMG, KCB (1840?–1841?), called one of the makers of New Japan, helped to draw up the Treaty of Tientsin in China; British Minister to Japan in 1865, the first white man to have audience of the Mikado; Minister to China in 1883; Minister Plenipotentiary to Japan in 1884

LIEUT.-GEN. SIR GORDON DOUGLAS PRITCHARD, KCB (1844–1851), served through the Indian Mutiny; in the China War led the assault on the North Taku Fort; Colonel Commanding the Royal Engineers

JOHN LAWRENCE TOOLE (1841–1845), one of the best-known Victorian actors; later produced several plays and burlesques at 'Toole's' Theatre in London

COL. T. D. SEWELL, FRAS (1841–1845), Grand Sword-bearer of England

SIR JOHN SEELEY (1846–1852), Composition Master at CLS; Professor of Latin, University College, London; Regius Professor of History, Cambridge University (where he is commemorated by the Seeley History Library); anonymous author of the controversial *Ecce Homo* (1865)

F. C. WACE (1846–1854), Fellow and Lecturer in Mathematics of St John's; Mayor of Cambridge

SIR HENRY EDMUND KNIGHT (1846–1849), Lord Mayor of London 1882–1883

REVD T. SKELTON, BD (1846–1853), Principal of Bishop's College, Calcutta; Canon of Southwell

WILLIAM CAWTHORNE UNWIN, LL.D, FRS (1848–1854), distinguished engineer whose striking achievement was harnessing the water-power of Niagara Falls for the provision of electricity; Emeritus Professor of City and Guilds of London Technical Institute; President of Engineering Section of the British Association and the Institute of Civil Engineers; member of the Council of the Royal Society

ERNEST A. HART, DCL (1848–1852), ophthalmic surgeon, editor of the *British Medical Journal*; Chairman of the Parliamentary Bills Committee of the British Medical Association

RT. HON. CHARLES THOMSON RITCHIE, 1st Baron Ritchie of Dundee (1849–1853), Conservative MP for Tower Hamlets 1874; Secretary to the Admiralty in Lord Salisbury's ministry of 1885; in 1886 became President of the Local Government Board; President of Board of Trade 1895, six years later Home Secretary; Chancellor of Exchequer in Balfour's Cabinet of 1902

EDWIN ABBOTT ABBOTT (1850–1857), Headmaster, CLS 1865-1889; English scholar, educationist, theologian; prolific and wide-ranging author

W. S. ALDIS (1851–1857), Principal of Auckland College, New Zealand; largely responsible for the admission of women to the Tripos at Cambridge

EDWARD DIVERS, FRS (1851–1852), Principal, Imperial College of Engineering, Japan

SIR WILLIAM HENRY PERKIN, LL.D, Ph.D, D.Sc, FRS (1851–1853), assistant to A. W. Hofman at Royal College of Chemistry; at the age of 18 discovered the mauve aniline dye which led to the foundation of the coal-tar industry; founder of organic chemistry in England; received large number of doctorates and scientific distinctions; President of the Chemical Society

REVD E. LEDGER (1851–1859), Fellow of Corpus Christi, Oxford; Professor of Astronomy at Gresham College

H. J. PURKISS (1852–1861), Principal of the Royal School of Naval Architecture; an out-standingly gifted mathematician who drowned in the Cam, aged 22

GENERAL SIR EDWARD STEDMAN, GCB, KCIE (1852–1859), Royal Artillery, took part in relief of Kandahar 1880, mentioned in dispatches; Inspector-General of Police in Burma 1886–1891; Quartermaster-General of India 1892–1895; Military Secretary to the India Office

REVD A. R. VARDY (1852–1860), Fellow of Trinity, Cambridge; returned to the school as a master from 1864 to 1872; Head Master of King Edward's, Birmingham

SIR NICHOLAS JOHN HANNEN (1856–1861), Chief Justice of the Supreme Court of China and Japan

S. S. BROWN (1854–1859), pioneer underwriter and manager of liability insurance; President of the Insurance Institute

E. LINLEY SAMBOURNE (1855–1856), chief cartoonist of *Punch*; his Chelsea home is preserved as a museum and headquarters of the Victorian Society

REVD H. P. GURNEY (1856–1866), the third successive Old Citizen (see W. S. Aldis and W. Garnett) to be Principl of Durham College of Science; killed in the Alps

SIR ALEXANDER PEDLER, CIE, FRS (1857–1865), Vice-Chancellor of the University of Calcutta

SIR ALEXANDER BLACKIE WILLIAM KENNEDY, LL.D, FRS (1858–1862), a distinguished and versatile engineer who was intimately associated with the development in England of electric lighting, trams, and railways; Professor of Engineering at University College, London; Chairman of the Admiralty Committee on Machinery Designs; Chairman of the Committee of Gun-Sights and Range-Finders during the War

CARLTON J. LAMBERT, FRAS (1858–1863), Fellow of Pembroke, Cambridge; Professor of Mathematics at the RNC Greenwich; founded the Lambert Scholarship at the School

A. D. CAREY (1859–1862), Collector of Salt Revenue in Bombay Presidency; in 1885-1886 he explored the River Tarim and Lake Lob Nor in Sinkiang, covering about 3000 miles in a little known part of Asia

THOMAS FISHER UNWIN (1859–1863), founded the publishing firm which bears his name; discovered the genius of Joseph Conrad and others; founder of the 'Mermaid' series of Elizabethan and Jacobean dramatists

REVD A. W. MOMERIE, D.Sc, LL.D (1860–1866), Fellow of St John's Cambridge; Professor of Logic and Metaphysics, King's College, London

PERCY GARDNER, FBA (1860–1862), Professor of Archaeology at Oxford and the Cambridge; authority on Greek art and numismatics; also wrote extensively on the New Testament and modernist religion

F. CLOWES (1861–1868), Professor of Chemistry, Nottingham University College

REVD PREB. WILSON CARLILE, CH (1860–1860), Founder of the Church Army

J. S. CURWEN (1861–1864), son of the inventor of the Tonic Sol-Fa system; editor of the *Musical Herald*

J. COX (1862–1871), Warden of Cavendish College, Cambridge; Professor of Physics, McGill University, Montreal

W. J. SOLLAS, LL.D, Sc.D, FRS (1863–1864), Fellow of St John's Cambridge, and University, Oxford; Professor of Geology and Palaeontology at Oxford

RT. HON. H. H. ASQUITH, KG (1864–1870), (first Earl of Oxford and Asquith) MP for East Fife 1886; Home Secretary 1892; Chancellor of the Exchequer 1905; Prime Minister 1908–1916; responsible for limiting the power of the House of Lords (1911) and declaring war on Germany (1914)

J. MORTIMER ANGUS (1864–1869) Professor of Latin and Registrar of the University of Wales

C. BENDALL (1864–1875), Professor of Sanskrit, Cambridge University

C. F. CROSS FRS (1864–1866), industrial chemist whose work on cellulose and viscose lead to the development of rayon and artificial silk

WILLIAM GARNETT (1864–1869), succeeded W. S. Aldis q. v. as Principal of Durham College of Science; Educational Adviser to the London County Council

TALBOT BAINES REED (1864–1866), author of school stories and founding publisher of the *Boys' Own Paper*; historian of printing

J. W. C. FEGAN (1865–1869), opened his first Boys' Home in Deptford when he was 19; devoted his life to work for the poor

L. R. FARNELL, FBA (1866–1874), Rector of Exeter College, Oxford; Vice-Chancellor, Oxford University; authority on Greek religion

SIR GEORGE NEWNES, Bart (1866), founded the *Westminster Gazette* and lighter periodicals; Liberal MP

A. H. BULLEN (1867–1875), scholar of Elizabethan poetry and drama, and rediscoverer of Thomas Campion; founded the Shakespeare Head Press; editor of *The Gentleman's Magazine*; Keeper of Printed Books at the British Museum

SIMEON JACOBS (1867–1872) Solicitor-General, Cape Colony

SIR GEORGE GOMME (1867–1875), Clerk to the London County Council; historian of London

A. GOODWIN (1867–1875), Professor of Latin, University College, London

W. BRAMWELL BOOTH, CH (1868–1868), second General of the Salvation Army

J. E. A. STEGGALL, LL.D (1868–1874), for fifty years Professor of Mathematics at University College, Dundee

RT. HON. ROBERT CHALMERS, GCB, 1st Baron Chalmers of Northiam (1870–1877), Chairman of the Board of Inland Revenue; Permanent Secretary of the Treasury; Governor of Ceylon; Master of Peterhouse, Cambridge; authority on the Pali language, and one of the few modern men to speak Latin fluently

SIR SIDNEY LEE, D.Litt, Litt.D, LL.D (1870–1878), one of the greatest of modern biographers and Shakespearians; editor with Sir Leslie Stephen of the *Dictionary of National Biography,* completed in 1891; author of *Life of Shakespeare*, at once acclaimed as the authoritative compendium of all that is known concerning the dramatist's life and work; Professor of English Literature in the University of London, at East London College; Fellow of the British Academy; Chairman of the Section on Medieval and Modern Philology and Literature

WILLIAM HENRY PERKIN LL.D, Sc.D, D.Sc, Ph.D, FRS (1870–1877), Waynflete Professor of Chemistry at Oxford; Fellow of Magdalene; recognised as 'the greatest organic chemist in England and one of the greatest in the world'

SIR FREDERICK GOWLAND HOPKINS, OM, D.Sc, LL.D, FRS (1871–1876), Discovered vitamins, thus founding the science of bio-chemistry; first Professor of Bio-Chemistry and creator of the Sir William Dunn Institute of Bio-Chemistry at Cambridge; Nobel Prize for Medicine in 1929; President of the Royal Society and the British Association; received the Royal Medal in 1918 and the Copley Medal in 1926

P. A. BARNETT (1872–1877), Professor of English, University College, Sheffield; Civil Adviser on Army Education

VERY REVD H. C. BEECHING (1872–1878), Professor of Pastoral Theology, King's College, London; Dean of Norwich; poet; literary editor of Shakespeare, Milton, Tennyson

ARTHUR GEORGE PERKIN, D.Sc, FRS (1872–1878), Emeritus Professor of Colour Chemistry and Dyeing; Dean of the Faculty of Technology, Leeds University

SIR WALTER RALEIGH (1874–1876), Professor of Modern Literature at Liverpool; Professor of English Literature at Glasgow and Oxford; author of many brilliant critical and biographical books, including *Style* (1897) and volumes on Milton, Wordsworth, Shakespeare, etc.

RT. REVD W. G. WHITTINGHAM, DD (1874–1876), Lord Bishop of St Edmundsbury and Ipswich

W. H. YOUNG Sc.D, D.Sc, FRS (1874–1881), Fellow of Peterhouse; Professor of Mathematics at the Universities of Calcutta, Liverpool, and Wales; President of the Union Internationale de Mathematiciens

G. A. J. COLE, FRS (1875–1877), Professor of Geology at the Royal College of Science, Dublin; Director of the Irish Geological Survey

R. S. CONWAY (1875–1883), Professor of Latin and Indo-European Philology, Manchester

H. T. DICKSEE (1875–1878), painter and etcher; became assistant to his father as Drawing Master at CLS in 1879, succeeding him in 1895

ERNEST GARDNER (1875–1880) (brother of Percy Gardner, q. v.), Director of the British School of Archaeology, Athens; Professor of Archaeology and Vice-Chancellor, London University; authority on Greek art and religion

SIR MALCOLM DELAVINGNE, KCB, KCVO (1877–1887), Deputy Permanent Under-Secretary, Home Office; a British representative at the 1919 Peace Conference, actively concerned with founding the International Labour Organisation, on whose Council he was British representative

STEWART MACPHERSON (1877–1880), Professor of Harmony and Composition at the Royal Academy of Music; Director of the Royal Philharmonic Society; Dean of the Faculty of Music at London University

SIR ISRAEL GOLLANCZ, FBA (1877–1882), First University Lecturer in English at Cambridge; Professor of English, London University; Shakespearian scholar and editor; Secretary of the British Academy

FRANK TILLYARD, CBE (1877–1883), Emeritus Professor of Commercial Law in the University of Birmingham; founder of the Poor Man's Society

W. S. LAZARUS-BARLOW, MD (1878–1884), Director of the Cancer Research Laboratories and Professor of Experimental Pathology at Middlesex Hospital; member of the Cancer Research Committee of the Board of Health

W. H. WAGSTAFF (1878–1885), Professor of Geometry, and senior Professor, at Gresham College

REVD T. B. HARDY, VC, DSO, MC (1879–1882), Head Master of Bentham Grammar School, Vicar of Hutton Roof, Kirkby Lonsdale; became an army Chaplain at the age of 52; Chaplain to the King; died of wounds shortly before the armistice

ARTHUR RACKHAM (1879–1883), well-known artist who illustrated many volumes of legends and fairytales

CHARLES EDWARD MONTAGUE, OBE (1879–1885), worked with C. P. Scott (his father-in-law) to raise the *Manchester Guardian* to a position unique in English journalism; author of influential leading articles, essays and novels, including *Disenchantment* (1922), a powerful denunciation of war, though he himself had shown much courage, enlisting at the age of 47

SIR THOMAS ARNOLD, CIE (1880–1883), Professor of Arabic, University College London; Educational Adviser to Indian Students; Hon. Fellow, Magdalene College

HON. SIR ANTON BERTRAM, KC (1881–1887), Attorney-General and later Chief Justice of Ceylon; Fellow of Caius

W. C. SUMMERS Litt.D (1881–1888), Fellow of St John's Cambridge; Emeritus Professor of Latin at Sheffield University

GEORGE WARRINGTON STEEVENS (1882–1888), Scholar of Balliol; Fellow of Pembroke, Oxford; before the Great War was considered the greatest of all war correspondents

RALPH PEACOCK (1883–1884), portrait painter

V. H. BLACKMAN, FRS (1884–1888), Professor of Botany, University of Leeds; Professor of Plant Physiology, Imperial College, London

C. S. MYERS, CBE, MD, Sc.D, D.Sc, FRS (1885–1890), one of the foremost British psychologists; Director of the Psychological Laboratory and Reader in Experimental Psychology at Cambridge; during the War Consulting Psychologist to the British Armies in France; Professor of Psychology at King's College, London

H. H. SCOTT, CMG, MD (1886–1891), Director of the Bureau of Hygiene and Tropical Diseases

H. M. RELTON (1887–1900), Professor of Dogmatic, Biblical and Historical Theology, University of London

E. S. COLLINS (1888–1890), succeeded his partner Ralph Knott (q. v.) as architect of the London County Hall

C. E. C. TATTERSALL (1888–1896), in charge of the Department of Textiles at the Victoria and Albert Museum

B. S. GLUCKSTEIN (1889–1893), one of ten family members at the School; founder of John Lyons & Co., caterers

H. J. THEODORE GODDARD (1889–1895); solicitor, legal advisor to Mrs Simpson (Duchess of Windsor) at the time of the Abdication

RALPH KNOTT (1889–1894), won the competition of the London County Council for the design of the new County Hall

HON. J. R. WOOD (1890–1897), Puisne Judge of the Supreme Court of Hong Kong

JACKSON DODDS, CBE (1892–1896), General manager, Bank of Montreal; First Deputy Chief Scout of Canada

RT. HON. EDWIN SAMUEL MONTAGU (1893–1895), Liberal MP for Chesterton; Private Secretary to the Chancellor of the Exchequer H. H. Asquith; Under-Secretary for India in 1910; Financial Secretary to the Treasury; Minister of Munitions and a member of the War Committee; Secretary of State for India; primarily responsible for the famous *Montagu-Chelmsford Report* on the government of India, following it up with the Government of India Act of 1919

G. ROTTER, GM, CB (1893–1898), Director of Explosives research, Royal Arsenal, Woolwich; awarded the George Medal for dismantling explosives during World War II

SIR CARLETON LANGLEY, QC (1884–1898), Attorney-General, Leeward Islands; Puisne Judge, British Guiana; Chief Justice, British Honduras

SIR MELLIS NAPIER, KCMG (1894–1895), Judge of Australian supreme court; Lieut.-Gov. and Chief Justice of South Australia; Chancellor, University of Adelaide

SIR HERMAN LEBUS, CBE (1895–1899), Chairman and Managing Director of Harris Lebus, furniture-makers

A. M. HIND (1895–1898), Keeper of Prints and Drawings at the British Museum; landscape painter; Slade Professor of Fine Arts at Oxford; Professor of Poetry at Harvard

SIR SAMUEL JOSEPH (1898–1903), Lord Mayor of London 1942–1943

L. A. WILLOUGHBY (1898–1900), Professor of German at Manchester University and University College, London; Gold Medallist of the Goethe Institute

J. C. CHAPMAN (1899–1905), Professor of Education, Yale University

SIR FREDERICK LEGGETT, KBE (1899–1902), Chief Industrial Commissioner and Deputy Permanent Secretary, Ministry of Labour

H. T. H. PIAGGIO (1899–1903), Professor of Mathematics, University of Nottingham, known as 'high-tension Henry'

R. A. FRAZER. FRS (1902–1909), Deputy Chief Scientific Officer, Aerodynamics Division, National Physical Laboratory

A. B. APPLETON (1903–1907), Professor of Anatomy, St Thomas's Hospital; Fellow of Downing College, Cambridge

SIDNEY SMITH (1904–1908), Hon. Fellow of Queens', Cambridge; author of the *Early History of Assyria*; Keeper of the Department of Egyptian and Assyrian Antiquities at the British Museum

SIR ALEXANDER DAVIDSON, KBE (1905–1912), Air Vice-Marshal

C. B. OLDMAN, CB, CVO (1905–1913), Principal Keeper of Printed Books, British Museum; wrote on Mozart

R. W. JAMES, FRS (1907–1909), Vice-Chancellor, University of Cape Town

S. I. LEVY, QC (1907–1909), Deputy Director, Ministry of Supply; Master of the Middle Temple

RT REVD D. L. REDDING (1907–1912), Bishop of Bunbury, Western Australia; Bishop Coadjutor, Melbourne

H. L. ROTH, D.Phil (1907–1915), Professor of Philosophy in the University of Jerusalem

RT. HON. VISCOUNT TENBY (Gwilym Lloyd-George) (1907–1910), Minister of Food and Power; Minister of Food; Home Secretary

MAX NEWMAN, FRS (1908–1915) (formerly Neumann), developed the first electronic computer (for decoding ciphers) at Bletchley Park during World War II; Fielden Professor of Mathematics, Manchester University

H. H. GATEIN (1909–1913), Professor of Commercial Law, Birmingham University

RT. HON. MALCOLM MACDONALD, OM, PC (1910–1911), High Commissioner, Canada; Governor-General, Malaya; High Commissioner, India; Governor-General and High Commissioner, Kenya; Chancellor, University of Durham

LIEUT.- COL. G. DE GRUCHY BARKAS, OBE, MC (1910–1913), Director of military camouflage in N. Africa in World War II (and so at El Alamein)

A. R. POWELL, FRS (1910–1913), Research Manager, Johnson Matthey Ltd

HENRY SHEREK (1910–1913), theatre impresario

R. S. STONELAY, FRS (1910–1912), Reader in Theoretical Geophysics, Cambridge University

R. K. CALLOW, FRS (1911–1919), bio-chemist who isolated vitamin D and synthesised cortisone

RT. REVD. S. A. ELEY (1911–1915), Bishop of Gibraltar

SIR GEOFFREY LAWRENCE, QC (1911–1921), Chairman, General Council of the Bar; Chairman, National Incomes Commission; High Court Judge

SIR MARRIOTT NICHOLLS (1911–1915), Dean of Medical School, St George's Hospital, London; Professor of Surgery, University of Khartoum

CECIL ROTH, Ph.D (1911–1917), wrote many works on Jewish and Florentine history

O. W. SNOW, OBE (1911–1919), Chief Scientist, Ministry of Agriculture, Ghana

A. BROTMAN (1912–1914), Secretary, Board of Deputies of British Jews

REVD SIR PERCY CHATTERTON, KBE, CMG (1912–1916), missionary, Papua New Guinea

A. ST G. HUGGETT, FRS (1912–1914), Professor of Physiology, St Mary's Hospital, London

J. O. IRWIN (1912–1918), President of Royal Statistical Society

ALEC COULSON (1912–1919), barrister; Chairman of the School's Committee and of the Board of Governors of CLS; Secretary of the John Carpenter Club for 51 years, then Honorary Life President

C. FOX (1913–1915), Professor of Mathematics, McGill University, Canada

SIR CYRIL HAWKER (1913–1918), President, MCC; Chairman of the Cricket Council

SIR HUGH LINSTEAD, OBE (1913–1917), MP for Putney; registrar/secretary, Pharmaceutical Society

R. W. SCARFF, CBE (1913–1918), Professor of Pathology, Middlesex Hospital

LORD (HORACE) EVANS, GCVO (1914–1920), physician to Queen Mary, King George VI, Queen Elizabeth II

SIR PATRICK LINSTEAD, FRS, CBE (1915–1919), Rector, Imperial College, London

W. G. MACLAGAN (1916–1922), Professor of Moral Philosophy, University of Glasgow

K. A. USHERWOOD, CBE (1916–1922), Chairman, Prudential Assurance Co.; President, Institute of Actuaries

LORD (ERIC) ASHBY OF BRANDON, FRS (1916–1923), Professor of Botany at University of Sydney and at Manchester University; Vice-Chancellor and then Chancellor of Queen's University, Belfast; Master of Clare College, Cambridge; Vice-Chancellor of Cambridge University

LEO GENN (1917–1924), film actor; prepared the indictment for the Belsen Camp Trial

SIR WYLIE MCKISSOCK, OBE (1917–1924), neurologist at St George's Hospital

D. E. RITCHIE (1917–1922), voice of 'Colonel Britton' during the War; introduced the 'V for Victory' slogan with its Morse code sign and the opening of Beethoven's 5th Symphony; later director of BBC European News and head of BBC publicity

REVD C. H. D. CULLINGFORD (1918–1923), Speleologist

S. R. SMITH, OBE (1918–1922), Secretary of the Corporation of Trinity House; Under-Secretary of State, Department of Health and Social Security

SIR GERALD GLOVER (1919–1924), property developer; racehorse owner (won the 1962 2000 Guineas with Privy Counsellor); philanthropist

D. H. MCLACHLAN, OBE (1919–1926), founding editor of the *Sunday Telegraph*

SIR JOHN DAVIS CVO (1920–1924), Chairman, Rank Organisation

SIR GEOFFREY ALDINGTON, KBE CMG (1921–1925), HM Ambassador to the Grand Duchy of Luxemburg

REVD PREB. D. M. LYNCH, CBE (1922–1930), Chief Secretary of the Church Army; Chaplain to the Queen

HAROLD ROSENTHAL, OBE (1922–1936), founding editor of *Opera* magazine

GP. CAPT. H. J. WILSON, AFC, CBE (1922–1925), World air speed record holder, 1945; chief test pilot, Farnborough

K. C. KING (1923–1930), Professor of German, King's College, London

LORD (VICTOR) MISHCON (1923–1933), first solicitor to be appointed honorary QC; Labour spokesman on legal affairs in House of Lords

L. G. THORNE (1923–1930), Principal, Guildhall School of Music and Drama

ERNEST LOUGH (1924–1929), as a treble in the Temple Church choir recorded Mendelssohn's 'Hear My Prayer' in 1927 (the first record to sell a million copies)

A. W. GAMINARA, CMG (1925–1932), Secretary of Kenneth Kaunda's cabinet in Zambia

LORD (DESMOND) HIRSHFIELD (1925–1929), founder of the Trades Union Trust

D. B. SCOTT (1925–1934) (formerly Schultz), worked at Bletchley Park decoding cyphers; founding Professor of Mathematics, Sussex University

P. C. FREEMAN, MC (1926–1935), international pistol and small-bore rifle shot

SIR FREDERICK MASON, KCVO, CMG (1927–1932), HM Ambassador, Chile

C. B. B. DOWNHAM (1928–1934), Professor of Physiology, Royal Free Hospital

J. FORD, GM (1928–1935), gazetted 1941 for defusing and removing an unexploded bomb lodged in a flue at Bexley Hospital (where he had gone as an outpatient)

COMPTE MAX LE MANSOIS-FIELD, OBE (1929–1940), chief interpreter, NATO

SIR DOUGLAS FRANK, QC (1930–1933), President of the Lands Tribunal

A. G. PERRIN (1930–1938), Governor, Reserve Bank of Malawi

W. B. YOUNG (1931–1935), Scottish rugby international; author under *nom de plume* 'Andrew Hamilton'

SIR KINGSLEY AMIS, CBE (1934–1941), author; many publications including *The Riverside Villas Murder* centred on a schoolboy attending 'Blackfriars Grammar'

DEREK ROY (1934–1937) (formerly Thomas), radio entertainer

W. A. CRADDOCK, LVO (1933–1939), Chairman and managing director, Harrods

DENIS NORDEN (1933–1938), radio and television scriptwriter and entertainer

P. I. ZETTER, CBE (1934–1940), Chairman, Zetters Pools; founder, Sports Aid Foundation; philanthropist

SIR GEORGE BLUNDEN (1935–1941), Deputy Governor, Bank of England; Chairman of the International Committee of Banking Supervisors

SIR LEO PLIATZKY (1935–1937), Second Permanent Secretary, Treasury; Permanent Secretary, Department of Trade

SIR PETER BALDWIN, KCB (1936–1941), Permanent Secretary, Department of Transport; President, Royal Society of Arts

J. E. FLOOD, OBE (1936–1942), Professor of Electrical Engineering and Pro Vice-Chancellor, University of Aston; member of the Monopolies and Mergers Commission

W. G. SPECTOR (1936–1941), Professor of Pathology, St Bartholomew's Hospital

J. W. THOMPSON (1936–1943), Professor of Pharmacology, University of Newcastle

P. H. NURSE (1937–1945), Professor of French, University of Kent

P. A. WAYMAN (1937–1945), Director, Dunsink Observatory, Dublin; Secretary of the International Astronomical Union

S. PREVEZER (1938–1948), Professor of Law, Sussex University

A. M. SIMONS, CMG (1938–1946), Head of UK delegation to UN Negotiations of Mutual Reduction of Forces and Armaments

SIR JOHN TITMAN, KCVO (1938–1940), Secretary, Lord Chamberlain's Office; Sergeant at Arms to HM Queen

P. R. WYCHERLEY, OBE (1938–1946), Director, King's Park and Botanic Garden, Perth, W. Australia

D. M. LEWIS (1939–1945), Professor of Ancient History, Oxford University

V. C. ABRAHAMS (1939–1945), Professor of Physiology, Ottawa University

I. M. GLYNN, FRS (1939–1946), Professor of Physiology, University of Cambridge

A. A. GLYNN (1939–1941), Professor of Bacteriology, St Mary's Hospital, London

LORD (GEOFFREY) FINSBERG (1940–1942), MP for Hampstead; Parliamentary Under Secretary, Department of the Environment; President, Council of Europe

JAMES CRESPI, QC (1941–1945), Recorder of Crown Court

K. C. H. SMITHIES (1941–1943), Judge of High Court

B. LESSEL (1943–1950), Professor of Pharmacy, London University

REVD B. E. BECK (1944–1952), Secretary, later President, Methodist Conference

R. L. BRAHAM (1945–1951), Professor of Paediatric Dentistry, University of California

LORD (FRANK) JUDD (1945–1953), Under-Secretary of State for the Royal Navy; MP for Portsmouth; Minister of State for Overseas Development; Director, Voluntary Service Overseas; Director-General, Oxfam

M. K. ADAMS (1946–1952), Air Vice-Marshal; test pilot

P. W. HAYES, FRS (1946–1950), Professor of Theoretical Physics, Edinburgh University

S. A. LEIGH (1947–1953), Real tennis doubles champion

LORD (ANTHONY) LESTER, QC (1947–1955), lawyer specialising in human rights; Recorder

M. G. J. NEARY (1948–1958), Organist and master of the choristers at Winchester Cathedral and at Westminster Abbey; President, Royal College of Organists

J. R. DE S. HONEY (1949–1952), Professor of Education at Rhodes University, Grahamstown, SA and at the University of Rhodesia; Professor of English Linguistics, Kuramoto University, Japan; Professor of English, Osaka International University, Japan

SIR PETER LEVENE, KBE (1951–1960), Head of Defence Procurement, Ministry of Defence; advisor to the Prime Minister on efficiency and effectiveness in the Civil Service

R. P. HARPER (1950–1958), Director, British School of Archaeology, Jerusalem

A. C. THISELTON (1950–1954), Principal of St John's College and Professor of Christian Theology

H. E. ETTINGHAUSEN (1951–1957), Professor of Spanish, Southampton University

MICHAEL APTED (1952–1960), film director

J. M. BREARLEY, OBE (1952–1960), Captain, Cambridge Cricket 1963, 1964; Captain of MCC 1977–1981; as Captain of England won 18 matches, drew 9 and lost 4

JONATHAN BARNES, FBA (1953–1960), Professor of Ancient Philosophy, Oxford University; Fellow of Balliol College

D. E. BLACKMAN (1953–1960), Professor of Psychology, Cardiff University

T. C. HALL (1955–1956), Professor of Horticulture, Wisconsin University

JULIAN BARNES (1957–1964), writer; books include *Metroland* (with many references to the life of a CLS sixth-former), *Flaubert's Parrot*, *A History of the World in 10$^1/_2$ Chapters*

C. S. H. HAMPTON (1957–1964), Eton fives amateur champion (with S. H. Courtney) 1969, 1970

M. C. WHITE (1957–1966), Professor of Postgraduate Medicine, Hull University

A. K. CAMPBELL (1958–1964), Professor of Medical Biochemistry, University of Wales

S. H. COURTNEY (1958–1968), public schools squash champion 1966, British junior squash champion 1967; Eton fives amateur champion (with C. S. H. Hampton) 1969, 1970

W. R. HARTSTON (1958–1965), British chess champion 1973, 1975; journalist and broadcaster

JOHN SHRAPNEL (1959–1961), actor

J. J. G. LAWDAY (1959–1966), British under-20 sabre champion 1966

S. W. TOLLIDAY (1960–1969), Professor of Economic and Social History, Leeds University; Professor of Economics, Harvard University

B. W. SILVERMAN (1961–1969), winner of British Mathematical Olympiad 1970; Professor of Statistics, University of Bath; Professor of Statistics, University of Bristol

STEVEN ISSERLIS (1969–1973), concert cellist

Y. COHEN (1972–1975), Professor of Economics, Rutgers University, New Jersey

P. KLENERMAN (1973–1981), British fencing team (sabre), Los Angeles Olympics

P.B. KRONHEIMER (1974–1980), Professor of Mathematics, Harvard University

N. G. B. EDWARDS (1977–1982), Scottish rugby international

KATHRYN J. STEVENS (1981–1983), British women's parachute champion 1986

M. T. HENNIGAN (1982–1989), world under-eighteen chess champion

List of Subscribers

NAME, *Status* (if not pupil), dates at School. Asterisk * indicates Chairman of Board of Governors

T. L. ADAM, 1945–1949

K. L. ADAMS, 1940–1948

A. C. ADONIS, 1992–

D. J. AGATE, 1944–1951

A. A. AHMED, 1994–

A. M. AHSAN, 1968–1976

E. D. ALDERMAN, 1989–

Mrs S. ALLEN, *Staff*, 1990–

C. N. L. ALLGROVE, 1988–1994

O. W. L. ALLGROVE, 1988–

D. AMES, 1923–1929

D. W. ANDERSON, 1932–1939

A. B. C. ANG, 1990–1995

W. ARMALY, 1994–

A. ARNOLD, 1992–

D. ASHMORE, 1952–1957,

R. C. ATTWOOD, 1946–1952

D. J. AYLETT, 1965–1972

N. AYTON, 1966–1975

R. J. BAILEY, *Staff*, 1970–

K. F. C. BAKER, 1953–1961

P. G. BALDWIN, 1953–1962

B. J. W. BALL, 1955–1960

H. D. BALLS*, 1934–1940, *Governor*, 1980–

M. H. BANBURY, 1955–1962

A. W. BANKS, 1933–1937

B. BARKER, 1994–

W. M. BARNES, 1990–

R. BARROW, *Staff*, 1968–1972

B. G. BASS, *Headmaster*, 1990–1995

R. T. BECK, *Governor*, 1971–1975

A. D. BELL, 1954–1961

L. BELL, 1942–1949

A. I. BENNETT, 1991–

I. J. BENNETT, 1946–1955

P. S. E. BENNETT, 1993–

S. BENTLEY, 1991–

M. A. BERK, 1994–

R. P. BERRY, 1991–

M. BETH, 1962–1967

S. BILES, 1978–1985

A. BIRTLES, 1951–1960

S. S. BLITZ, 1940–1948

G. BLUNDEN, 1935–1941

J. BOHM, 1994–

M. A. H. BOND, 1947–1956

J. A. BOYES, *Headmaster*, 1965–1984

R. L. BRAHAM, 1945–1951

G. R. BREED, 1935–1942

P. E. A. BROOKHOUSE, 1932–1937

P. M. BROWN, 1958–1967

F. F. BRUNDLE, 1924–1932

N. J. BRUNSKILL, 1993–1995

K. J. BURRASTON, 1933–1940

S. D. P. BURSTIN, 1990–

P. J. BUTT, *Staff*, 1974–

A. K. CAMPBELL, 1958–1964

P. CANDEGGI, 1990–

H. A. CAPPER, 1929–1931

R. E. CAPPER, 1957–1966

W. A. CARNEY, 1930–1934

A. A. CARTER, *Staff*, 1974–1981

S. N. CASS, 1976–1980

B. F. CATT, *Governor*, 1985–

T. E. CATTERMOLE, 1991–

G. H. CHALLIS, *Governor*, 1991–

J. CHALSTREY, *Governor*, 1981–1984

J. R. CHALSTREY, 1973–1980

A. C. CHANDLER, 1960–1967

E. CHAPMAN, 1979–1984

F. B. CHARATAN, 1934–1939

G. D. CHARATAN, 1942–1948

Miss E. F. CHARTINIER, *Staff*, 1991–1994

J. C. C. CHAU, 1989–

A. CHKLAR, 1991–

J. CHURCHMAN, 1959–1966

C. D. CHUTE, 1990–

F. J. CHUTE, *Staff*, 1988–

M. R. A. COFFEY, 1992–

J. E. COHEN, 1970–1977

P. L. G. COLE, 1931–1937

I. R. COLLINS, 1952–1959

N. COLLINS, 1993–

Z. B. H. COOPER, 1988–1995

M. J. COOTER, 1989–

S. M. COOTER, 1988–1994

J. H. CORDLE, 1925–1930

M. COREN, 1975–1982

M. F. CORNISH, *Staff*, 1948–1974

P. A. CORNISH, 1962–1971

G. R. CORT, *Staff*, 1981–

S. COURTNEY, 1958–1968

W. A. CRADDOCK, 1933–1939

G. D. CRANE, 1944–1952

T. CREASEY, 1948–1950

B. E. CREED, 1955–1964

P. A. CROSS, 1954–1961

R. M. DANCEY, *Headmaster*, 1995–

K. R. K. DAVIES, 1972–1980

D. A. DAVIS, 1983–1990

N. DAVIS, 1985–1994

W. D. DAVIS, 1987–1994

R. S. DAWE, 1954–1959

B. R. DAY, 1950–1956

B. DE THAME, 1937–1941

E. H. L. DEVEREUX, 1947–1955

R. DILMAGHANIAN, 1980–1985

P. K. DONALDSON, 1941–1950

K. A. DONALLY, 1970–1975

G. R. DOWSON, 1936–1938

J. DUDLEY, 1936–1940

M. C. DYER, 1958–1965

D. W. DYKE, *Staff*, 1975–

MISS J. EASON, *Staff*, 1968–1994

D. A. EDDY, 1949–1956

R. H. EDMONDSON, 1963–1967

R. H. EDMONDSON, 1963–1968

R. J. A. EDWARDS, *Staff*, 1966–

M. EGNER, 1990–

B. H. ELLIS, 1934–1942

J. G. EMERSON, 1960–1967

R. A. ENGLAND, *Staff*, 1968–1989

M. C. EVANS, 1962–1968

S. FAIRBOTHAM, 1949–1953

H. FARRAR, 1928–1932

B. FARTHING*, *Governor*, 1983–

R. FEARN, 1993–

J. A. FELL*, *Governor*, 1983–

G. FINSBERG, 1940–1942

R. FISCHEL, 1962–1971

J. E. FLOOD, 1936–1942

A. J. G. FORSTER, 1958–1964

R. D. FOX, 1958–1964

N. L. FRASER, 1971–1978

R. L. FRASER, 1973–1978

S. L. FREEBERNE, 1994–

J. FYSON, 1936–1941

J. W. GARDNER, 1924–1930

T. GARTSIDE, 1939–1947

L. P. GIBBONS, *Staff*, 1994–

J. GIBILARO, 1992–

D. GIBSON, 1079–1985

G. GILBEY, 1944–1950

N. GILL, 1993–

L. A. M. GINGER, 1918–1920

I. GLEISER, 1959–1966

B. D. GOLD, 1992–

C. J. GOODERIDGE, 1954–1962

A. W. GOULD, *Staff*, 1971–1994

J. H. GRACEY, 1935–1942

A. GRAHAM, *Governor*, 1983–1985

D. L. GRANT, 1993–

G. E. T. GRANTER, 1945–1955

R. C. M. GREEN, 1936–1942

N. GREENHALGH, 1993–

G. S. GRIFFIN, *Staff*, 1981–

R. P. F. GRIFFITHS, 1956–1963

P. GRIFFITS, 1931–1936

D. GROSSEL, *Staff*, 1990–

J. GRUDER, 1966–1972

P. A. R. GULVANESSIAN, 1987–1994

D. C. HADJIPATERAS, 1968–1970

B. W. G. M. HALL, 1994–

W. HALLETT, *Head Porter*, 1982–

J. M. HAMMOND, *Headmaster*, 1984–1990

C. S. H. HAMPTON, 1958–1964

B. J. HARDING, 1944–1949

B. HARRADINE, 1938–1944

K. B. HARRIS, 1963–1969

P. M. D. HARRIS, 1973–1979

P. R. HARRISON, 1942–1947

A. E. HART, *Staff*, 1968–1988

E. M. HATLEY, *Bursar*, 1995–

H. P. HAWKEN, 1930–1936

T. J. HEARD, 1953–1959, *Staff*, 1967–, *Second Master*, 1980–

R. P. HEDLEY, 1931–1938

F. W. HELYAR, 1939–1944

D. R. HEMINWAY, *Staff*, 1985–

D. HENNIGAN, 1989–

M. HENNIGAN, 1982–1989

P. HENNIGAN, 1984–1991

S. HENNIGAN, 1990–

J. M. HILDITCH, 1953–1961

D. A. HILLMAN, *Staff*, 1971–1985

R. HILLMAN, 1986–1993

W. HILLMAN, 1954–1961

M. D. HIND, 1951–1956

P. HIND, 1960–1966

J. J. HINTON, 1981–1986

N. HIRSHFIELD, 1924–1929

A. HODGES, 1947–1951

M. J. G. HOME, 1962–1966

J. R. DE S. HONEY, 1949–1952

J. A. G. HOPKINS, 1944–1952

C. HORN, 1961–1966

N. HUNNINGS, 1939–1948

G. T. HUTTON, 1944–1951

J. H. HUTTON, 1975–1979

M. HUXHAM, 1993–

D. J. ISAACS, 1940–1944

R. K. ISAACS, 1944–1951

M. ISRAEL, 1965–1973

B. J. JACKSON, 1929–1938

M. JACOBS, 1970–1978

A. JAHANGIR, 1992–

J. B. JAMES, 1944–1950

W. JENKINS, 1992–

G. JIGGENS, 1990–

P. JIGGENS, 1993–

V. JOFFE, 1963–1969,

A. S. JOHN, 1986–1989

D. JOHN, 1980–1987

O. C. JOHN, 1987–

P. H. L. JOHNSON, 1944–1949

T. T. R. JOHNSON, 1946–1953

R. E. JOHNSTON, 1924–1930

C. N. JONES, 1937–1942

P. JONES, 1938–1946

D. KAHYA, 1993–

R. KAY, 1989–1994

S. E. KAY, 1994–

J. KEDDIE, 1989–

G. F. M. KELLETT, 1989–1991

MRS M. W. F. KELLETT, *Governor*, 1989–

D. KEMP, *Governor*, 1985–

S. J. KERN, 1961–1968

G. B. KESSLER, 1964–1971

S. K. KETTNER, 1986–1994

R. M. KINCHIN-SMITH, 1973–1976

J. R. KING, 1945–1949

A. KINGSLEY, 1977–1984

J. KLEIN, 1980–1987

J. W. KLUGER, 1958–1966

L. A. KNIGHT, 1953–1959, *Staff*, 1969–

H. KNORPEL, 1934–1942

D. W. KNOX, 1956–1965

D. L. KOEKOEK, 1993–

J. R. KROPMAN, 1969–1975

R. A. J. KUMAR, 1994–

P. F. LACAMP, 1951–1959

J. LACK, 1971–1977

P. LANDAU, 1988–1993

B. W. LANDERS, 1930–1938

D. W. LANGLEY, 1923–1926

D. F. LATHAM, 1930–1936

A. LAUFFER, 1992–

J. LAUFFER, 1966–1972, *Staff*, 1978–1988

D. LAWSON, 1944–1952

D. I. LEADBETTER, 1986–1994

D. J. LEAPMAN, 1932–1941

J. R. LEIGH, 1946–1953

A. LEITHEAD, 1990–

H. LEITHEAD, 1991–

J. LEITHEAD, 1994–

R. LERNER, 1993–

D. D. A. LESLIE, 1958–1963

P. LEVENE, 1951–1960, *Governor*, 1984–

L. LEVENTHAL, 1992–

E. B. LEVIN, 1948–1955

M. LEVY-ANDERSON, 1993–

J. LEWIS, 1963–1971

S. LEWIS, 1972–1980

J. D. LIGGINS, 1946–1953

J. LONGHURST, 1973–1981

D. J. LOOSEMORE, 1953–1963

K. M. LOUKES, 1960–1967

S. M. LOUKES, 1988–1995

R. J. LYGOE, 1985–1992

D. M. LYNCH, 1922–1930

P. J. E. MACE, 1962–1970

A. MACKIE, 1978–1980

A. E. MANLY, 1933–1939

A. R. MANLY, 1934–1939

A. S. MANN, 1976–1983

S. M. MANNING, 1979–1987

R. P. MARION, 1968–1973

S. D. MARKHAM, 1992–

J. E. B. MARSH, *Staff*, 1932–1972

W. D. MARSH, 1946–1950

M. J. A. MARTIN, 1992–

G. J. MATTHEWS, 1957–1966

J. S. N. MAYES, 1988–1995

P. B. MAYHEW, 1944–1952

R. McDONAGH, 1994–

P. J. McDONOUGH, *Staff*, 1988–

D. McGINTY, 1966–1973

J. M. McKEAND, 1948–1952

D. J. McLAREN, 1994–

J. W. MEAD, 1925–1929

T. E. MEDDINGS, 1932–1938

G. J. MELMOTH, 1948–1957

A. D. MEMBREY, 1989–

J. I. METCALFE, 1938–1948

A. J. MEZZETTI, 1953–1962

P. R. MILLER, 1967–1973

S. I. MILLMAN, 1960–1966

N. J. MITCHINSON, 1955–1962

D. MONAGHAN, 1969–1975

J. MOORE, 1919–1924

W. D. H. MOORE, *Staff*, 1950–1980, *Second Master*, 1968–1980

K. I. MORELL, 1933–1939

P. MORGAN, 1965–1973

D. MORGANSTEIN, 1983–1991

K. W. MORRIS, 1931–1938

G. A. D. MOSS, 1928–1932

K. H. MOSTYN, 1924–1934

F. M. MUGHAL, 1991–

R. MUKHERJEE, 1987–1994

D. MUNNS, 1929–1937

S. J. MURPHY, 1944–1950

A. V. M. MURRAY, *Staff*, 1967–1981

D. NADER, 1993–

A. NEVILLE, 1993–

P. NEWMAN, 1968–1974

P. NICOLAOU, 1989–1994

MRS L. O'CONNOR, *Staff*, 1969–1986

A. O'SULLIVAN, *Staff*, 1988–

G. O'SULLIVAN, 1988–1995

R. O'SULLIVAN, 1990–1992

D. L. PARKER, 1949–1958

I. D. PARKER, 1960–1968

J. C. PARKER, 1948–1954

G. H. PARKINSON, 1946–1952

A. A. PATEL, 1985–1992

M. PATERNOTT, *Staff*, 1994–

G. PATOU, 1971–1976

D. J. PATTERSON, 1983–1989

R. J. PATTERSON, 1985–1992

B. PEARCE, 1949–1953

D. J. M. PEARSON, 1993–

M. PEEL, 1981–1987

T. M. PELTA, 1990–

D. L. PENN, 1974–1980

D. W. PEPPER, 1988–

A. G. PERRIN, 1930–1938

J. E. PETERS, 1988–1993

J. G. PETT, 1973–1980

G. PHILLIPSON, *Staff*, 1987–

L. PITCHER, 1987–1994

G. A. C. PITT, 1922–1929

G. L. B. PITT, 1930–1938

R. G. POMEROY, *Staff*, 1975–

A. PORTER, 1991–

R. M. W. PORTER, 1944–1949

A. S. POTTERSMAN, 1948–1958

F. E. POWELL, 1926–1931

A. PREMATCHANDRA, 1978–1984

P. PREMATCHANDRA, 1979–1986

R. J. K. PRESCOTT, 1983–1991

T. A. K. PRESCOTT, 1987–1994

T. PRITCHARD, 1993–

G. RACE, 1991–

R. G. RADFORD, 1955–1963

C. J. RAE, 1948–1955

R. A. RAEBURN, 1973–1981

A. RAISSI-DEHKORDY, 1988–

S. RAJAK, 1987–1992

I. RAPPAPORT, 1958–1965

R. A. RATNER*, *Governor*, 1982–1991

J. B. READ, 1963–1971

M. S. M. READ, 1944–1950

T. R. A. READER, *Staff*, 1977–

N. G. REEVES, 1926–1932

T. J. REISNER, 1987–1994

C. RHODES, 1988–

D. G. RICE, 1937–1946

D. G. RICE, 1958–1965

J. H. C. RICHARDSON, 1937–1942

S. RICKARD, 1993–

M. H. RITCHLEY, 1957–1964

D. RITMAN, 1988–1995

J. E. RIX, 1950–1957

C. ROBERTS, 1992–

E. K. ROBERTS, 1927–1932

B. A. ROGERS, 1990–

T. ROLL-PICKERING, 1994–

R. D. ROMAIN, 1971–1976

A. ROSE, 1938–1943

O. ROSENBERG, 1994–

A. ROTSEY, 1993–

M. L. RUSSELL, 1991–

G. RYDER, *Staff*, 1970–1990

D. S. SACH, 1959–1968

K. S. SAGER, 1993–

A. P. L. SALMON, 1986–1989

D. G. SALTER, 1994–

M. J. SANT, *Bursar*, 1993–1995

C. F. SAUNDERS, 1928–1933

D. A. SCALES, 1957–1965

K. SCHREIBER, 1958–1963

R. M. SCOTT, 1947–1956

B. SEAGER, *Staff*, 1981–1989

S. A. SELLON, *Governor*, 1992–

T. F. SEWRY, 1991–

B. A. SHADDICK, 1941–1949

N. P. N. SHAH, 1990–

S. SHAPIRO, 1972–1977

B. J. SHARP, 1952–1959

R. G. SHILLINGFORD, *Governor*, 1961–1974

L. S. J. SHIPP, 1940–1945

M. A. SHIRE, 1994–

S. SHORVON, 1960–1965

M. SIGNY, 1966–1971

J. T. R. SILVERMAN, 1959–1967

A. M. SIMONS, 1938–1946

N. D. SIMONS, 1942–1947

J. SIMPSON, 1991–

J. R. SIMPSON, 1947–1955

H. SINGH, 1991–

T. SINGH, 1992–

D. St. B. SLADEN, 1945–1948

C. J. SMITH, *Staff*, 1985–

G. W. SMITH, 1912–1917

J. G. A. SMITH, 1936–1941

A. SOFRONIOU, 1994–

N. P. SOUTHEY, 1948–1953

S. SOVIN, 1944–1953

N. STEIN, 1987–1994

P. STEIN, 1990–

K. G. STELLA, 1965–1972

D. R, STENHOUSE, *Bursar*, 1960–1978

M. J. STEPHENSON, 1971–1977

M. J. STEVENS, 1949–1957

P. K. STEVENSON, 1931–1938

P. E. STILES, 1957–1964

M. D. STOCK, 1992–

V. N. STOCKTON, 1940–1945

A. E. W. STORMER, 1952–1957

K. G. H. STUBBS, 1962–1968

A. R. W. SWAN, 1967–1970

R. K. SWAN, 1930–1935

A. SZCZERBIUK, 1990–

J. C. TADMAN, 1946–1950

Mrs H. TAKADA, *Staff*, 1991–

D. R. TAUNT, 1931–1936

A. E. TAYLOR, 1993–

D. TAYLOR, 1991–

M. A. TAYLOR, 1978–1985

M. W. THOMAS, 1953–1960

R. A. THOMAS, 1994–

R. E. THOMAS, 1955–1962

J. W. THOMPSON, 1936–1943

C. A. J. THOMSON, 1983–1990

B. H. TINTON, 1934–1938

C. N. K. TIZARD, 1944–1952

C. TOWNSEND, 1955–1962

J. E. TREVERTON, 1944–1948

M. A. R. TUCK, 1948–1956

A. F. TUCKER, 1950–1958

P. TURL, 1941–1951

Mrs P. C. USHER, *Staff*, 1992–

I. VAN RITCHIE, 1994–

C. VERRALL, 1955–1962

S. VISCHER, 1994–

C. N. VOKINS, *Staff*, 1926–1968

B. N. WALKER, 1994–

D. WALKER, 1967–1974

S. WALSH, *Governor*, 1991–

J. R. WALTERS, 1964–1968

B. C. WARD, 1956–1960

B. W. WATERS, 1947–1954

J. P. C. WATKINS, 1963–1971

R. C. WATSON, 1915–1920

P. A. WAYMAN, 1937–1945

A. J. C. WEILL, 1948–1955

G. S. C. WEILL, 1960–1968

J. WESTBURY, 1987–1994

L. WESTBURY, 1992–

C. D. WEYMAN, 1948–1954

D. F. WHEAT, 1921–1924

P. J. S. WHITMORE, *Staff*, 1954–1981

B. J. WHITNEY, 1944–1950

P. L. WICKHAM, 1957–1966

G. W. F. WILDE, 1962–1969

C. WILLIAMS, 1992–

A. WILLIS, 1961–1968

D. V. WILLSMORE, 1937–1944

R. T. D. WILMOT, *Governor*, 1987–

K. WILSON, 1957–1964

D. WITKIN, 1989–1994

J. F. WOOD, 1969–1976

C. J. WOODBRIDGE, 1951–1958

P. WOODCOCK, 1949–1958

D. A. WRIGHT, 1992–

K. G. WRIGHT, 1944–1950

P. WYCHERLEY, 1938–1946

M. A. YOUNG, 1945–1952

W. B. YOUNG, 1930–1935

U. D. ZARFATY, 1988–

A. ZELLICK, 1990–

N. J. ZIMAN, 1954–1963

Index